Sunday Missal for Young Catholics 2011

I want to know Jesus better.

This missal will help you take part in the Mass on Sundays and important feast days. Pages 2 to 32 contain the words and explain the gestures that are the same for every Mass. The rest of the book gives you the readings and prayers for each Sunday of the year.

Look over the readings with your family before you go to church. This is an excellent way to use this book and a wonderful way to prepare for Mass.

The most important thing about this little book is that it will help you to *know Jesus better*. Jesus came to bring God's love into the world. And his Spirit continues to fill us with love for one another.

We hope the short notes in this book will help you to participate more fully in the Mass. May the Mass become an important part of your life as you grow up, and may the readings and prayers you find in this missal inspire you to love and serve others just as Jesus did.

What we need to celebrate the Mass

A **priest** who makes Jesus present and acts in his name.

A group of Christians. You are a Christian by your baptism.

Books with prayers (the missal) and readings (the lectionary).

The **altar** is the table where the priest consecrates bread and wine.

Holy vessels
chalice   ciborium   paten

Two **cruets**, or small glass containers, one full of water, and the other full of wine.

The **ambo** is the place where the Word of God is proclaimed.

Bread and wine
The Mass is the commemoration of what Jesus did during the Last Supper with his disciples, before he died. The bread is shaped like a small disk and is called a "host."

The four main parts of the Mass

On the following pages you will find the words that the priest says and the responses we say together during each part of the Mass. You will also find explanations and responses to many questions that people ask about the Mass.

Gathering Prayers

The Lord brings us together.
We ask God for forgiveness.
We give glory to God.

The Word

We listen to the Word of God.
We proclaim our faith.
We pray for the whole world.

The Eucharist

We offer bread and wine to God.
We give thanks to God.
We say the Lord's Prayer.
We share the peace of Christ.
We receive Jesus in communion.

Sending Forth

The Lord sends us home to live the Gospel.

The Lord brings us together

We come together in church with family, friends, neighbours, and strangers. We are here because Jesus has invited us to be here.

When the priest comes in, we stand up and sing. Then we make the sign of the cross along with the priest.

Priest: In the name of the Father, and of the Son, and of the Holy Spirit.

Everyone: Amen.

Sometimes, the words can change a bit, but usually the priest will say:

Priest: The grace of our Lord Jesus Christ and the love of God and the fellowship of the Holy Spirit be with you all.

Everyone: And also with you.

Why do we celebrate Mass on Sunday?

Jesus rose from the dead on Sunday, the day after the Sabbath. That is why Christians get together with Jesus on that day. Over time, people started to call it "the day of the Lord."

Why do we celebrate Mass in a church?

Churches are built specially for Christians to gather in. If needed, Mass can be celebrated in other places: a home, a school, a plaza, a jail, a hospital, a park…

Why do we need a priest to celebrate Mass?

We believe that Jesus is present in the person of the priest when Christians gather for the Mass. He presides over the celebration of the Lord's supper in the name of Jesus Christ.

Gestures

Standing up

We stand to welcome Jesus who is present among us when we gather in his name.

The sign of the cross

With our right hand we make the sign of the cross (from our forehead, to our chest, from our left shoulder to our right) and say "In the name of the Father, and of the Son, and of the Holy Spirit." This is how all Catholic prayer begins.

Singing

This is a joyful way to pray together.

5

We ask God for forgiveness

We speak to God and we recognize that we have done wrong. We ask forgiveness for our misdeeds. God, who knows and loves us, forgives us.

Priest: My brothers and sisters, to prepare ourselves to celebrate the sacred mysteries, let us call to mind our sins.

We silently recognize our faults and allow God's loving forgiveness to touch us.

Everyone: I confess to almighty God, and to you, my brothers and sisters, that I have sinned through my own fault, in my thoughts and in my words, in what I have done, and in what I have failed to do; and I ask blessed Mary, ever virgin, all the angels and saints, and you, my brothers and sisters, to pray for me to the Lord our God.

Priest: May almighty God have mercy on us, forgive us our sins, and bring us to everlasting life.

Everyone: Amen.

Priest: Lord, have mercy.

Everyone: Lord, have mercy.

Priest: Christ, have mercy.

Everyone: Christ, have mercy.

Priest: Lord, have mercy.

Everyone: Lord, have mercy.

Confess

We recognize before others that we have turned away from God, who is love.

Mercy

We know God is full of mercy —that he loves us even when we have sinned. God's mercy is always there for us.

Amen

This is a Hebrew word meaning "Yes, I agree. I commit myself."

Lord

This is a name that we give to God. Christians call Jesus "Lord" because we believe he is the Son of God.

Christ or Messiah

In the Bible, these words designate someone who has been blessed with perfumed oil. This blessing is a sign that God has given a mission to the person. Christians give this name to Jesus.

Tapping our heart

This is a way of saying we are very sorry for our sins.

We give glory to God

We recognize God's greatness when we say "Glory to God." This prayer begins with the hymn the angels sang when they announced Jesus' birth to the shepherds.

Everyone: Glory to God in the highest,
and peace to his people on earth.

Lord God, heavenly King,
almighty God and Father,
we worship you,
we give you thanks,
we praise you for your glory.

Lord Jesus Christ, only Son of the Father,
Lord God, Lamb of God,
you take away the sin of the world:
have mercy on us;
you are seated at the right hand of the Father:
receive our prayer.

For you alone are the Holy One,
you alone are the Lord,
you alone are the Most High, Jesus Christ,
with the Holy Spirit,
in the glory of God the Father. Amen.

Priest: Let us pray.

The priest invites us to pray. He then says a prayer in the name of all of us, and finishes like this:

We ask this through our Lord Jesus Christ, your Son, who lives and reigns with you and with the Holy Spirit, one God, for ever and ever.

Everyone: Amen.

Glory

With this word, we indicate the greatness of a person. It shows that a person is important. When we say "Glory to God" we are recognizing that God is important in our lives.

Almighty

When we say that God is almighty, we mean that nothing is impossible for God.

Praise

To praise is to speak well and enthusiastically of someone.

Sin of the world

This expression refers to all the evil that is done in the world.

Holy Spirit

This is the Spirit of God, our heavenly Guide, who fills us with love for Jesus.

We listen to the Word of God

This is the moment when we listen to several texts from the Bible. We welcome God who speaks to us today.

You can follow the texts that are read in this book. Look for the Sunday that corresponds to today's date.

The first two readings

We sit down for these readings. The first reading is usually taken from the Old Testament. The second is from a letter written by an apostle to the first Christians. Between these two readings, we pray with the responsorial psalm, which we do best when it is sung.

The Gospel

We stand and sing Alleluia! as we prepare to listen carefully to a reading from one of the gospels.

Priest: The Lord be with you.

Everyone: And also with you.

Priest: A reading from the holy Gospel according to N.

Everyone: Glory to you, Lord.

We trace three crosses with our thumb: one on our forehead, one on our lips, and another on our heart. When the reading is finished, the priest kisses the book and says:

Priest: The Gospel of the Lord.

Everyone: Praise to you, Lord Jesus Christ.

Homily

We sit down to listen to the comments of the priest, which help us to understand and apply the Word of God in our lives.

What does it mean?

Bible

This is the holy book of all Christians. The Old Testament tells the story of the Covenant God made with the Jewish people before Jesus' time. The New Testament tells the story of the Covenant God made with all people through his son Jesus Christ.

Psalm

The psalms are prayers that are found in the Bible. They are songs.

Alleluia!

This Hebrew word means "May God be praised and thanked."

Gospel

The word "gospel" means "good news." Jesus himself is the Good News who lives with us. The first four books of the New Testament are called "gospels." They transmit the good news to us.

Gestures

The sign of the cross which we make on our forehead, lips and heart

means that we want to make the gospel so much a part of our life that we can proclaim it to all around us with all our heart.

Kissing the book of the Gospels

When the priest does this, he says in a low voice: "May the words of the gospel wipe away our sins."

We proclaim our faith

We have just listened to the Word of God. To respond to it, with all other Christians in the world, we proclaim the "Creed."

We stand up and proclaim our faith:

Everyone: I believe in God, the Father almighty,
  creator of heaven and earth.

I believe in Jesus Christ, his only Son, our Lord.
He was conceived by the power of the Holy Spirit
  and born of the Virgin Mary.
He suffered under Pontius Pilate,
  was crucified, died, and was buried.
He descended to the dead.
On the third day he rose again.
He ascended into heaven,
  and is seated at the right hand of the Father.
He will come again to judge the living and the dead.

I believe in the Holy Spirit,
  the holy catholic Church,
  the communion of saints,
  the forgiveness of sins,
  the resurrection of the body,
  and the life everlasting.
  Amen.

What does it mean?

Creed

From the Latin verb *credo* that means "I believe." The Creed is the prayer that expresses our faith as Christians.

He suffered

Means the torture Jesus endured before he died on the cross.

Pontius Pilate

This is the name of the Roman governor who ordered that Jesus be crucified.

Crucified

Jesus died by crucifixion. He was nailed to a cross.

Catholic

In Greek, this word means "universal." The Church is open to all people in the world.

Church

The "Church" with a big C refers to the whole Christian community throughout the world. The "church" with a little c is a building where we go to worship God.

Resurrection

Means coming back to life after having died. God raised Jesus from the dead and gave him new life for ever. Jesus shares that life with us.

We pray for the whole world

This is the moment of the universal Prayer of the Faithful when we present our petitions to God. We pray for the Church, for all of humanity, for those who are sick or lonely, for children who are abandoned, for those who suffer through natural disasters...

After each petition we respond with a phrase, such as:

Everyone: Lord, hear our prayer.

Reader: For the needs of the Church, ...

For peace in every country, ...

For the hungry and the homeless, ...

For ourselves and for all God's children, ...

Priest: You are our God and we are your People. Hear the prayers that come from our hearts. Open before us the path of life. Send your Spirit to guide us and to help us work for your kingdom.

Everyone: Amen.

What does it mean?

Kingdom

The kingdom of God is not a country. It is life with God that Jesus brings us. We show we love God by the way we love each other.

Some questions

Why do we call the Prayer of the Faithful "universal"?

It is a universal prayer because it includes everyone: we pray to God for ourselves, for those who are close to us, and for all the people of the world.

Why do we take up a collection?

Christians help out with the maintenance of the church building, and also help people who are in need.

GENINA

We offer bread and wine to God

The celebration of the Lord's Supper continues at the altar. The priest presents the bread and wine to God and we bless God with him.

We sit down. The priest takes the bread and wine, and lifts them up, saying:

Priest: Blessed are you, Lord, God of all creation. Through your goodness we have this bread to offer, which earth has given and human hands have made. It will become for us the bread of life.

Everyone: Blessed be God for ever.

Priest: Blessed are you, Lord, God of all creation. Through your goodness we have this wine to offer, fruit of the vine and work of human hands. It will become our spiritual drink.

Everyone: Blessed be God for ever.

The priest washes his hands and says:

Priest: Pray, friends, that our sacrifice may be acceptable to God, the almighty Father.

Everyone: May the Lord accept the sacrifice at your hands for the praise and glory of his name, for our good, and the good of all his Church.

We stand while the priest, with hands extended, says a prayer over the bread and wine. He usually ends the prayer by saying:

Priest: We ask this in the name of Jesus the Lord.

Everyone: Amen.

What does it mean?

Eucharist

A Greek word that means "gratefulness, thanksgiving." The Mass is also called the Eucharist.

Blessed

To bless means to speak well of someone. To bless God is to give thanks for everything God gives us.

Sacrifice

God does not ask for animal sacrifice, as in the old days. Nor does God ask us to die on a cross, like Jesus did. Instead, God asks us to offer our daily life, with Jesus, as a beautiful gift.

Gestures

Procession with the bread and the wine

With this gesture we present to God the fruit of our work and we give thanks for the gift of life that comes from God.

Drops of water in the wine

With this sign, the priest prays that our life be united with God's life.

Washing of hands

Before saying the most important prayer of the Mass, the priest washes his hands and asks God to wash away his sins.

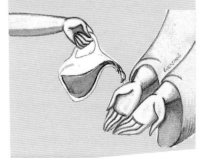

We give thanks to God

At this moment we give thanks to God for his Son, Jesus Christ, for life, and for all that he gives us. This is how the great Eucharistic Prayer begins.

Priest: The Lord be with you.

Everyone: And also with you.

Priest: Lift up your hearts.

Everyone: We lift them up to the Lord.

Priest: Let us give thanks to the Lord our God.

Everyone: It is right to give him thanks and praise.

Here is one way of celebrating the Eucharist with young Catholics. On page 21, you will find Eucharistic Prayer II which is a common way of celebrating the Eucharist with grown-ups.

Eucharistic Prayer for Mass with Children I

Priest: God our Father, you have brought us here together so that we can give you thanks and praise for all the wonderful things you have done.

We thank you for all that is beautiful in the world and for the happiness you have given us. We praise you for daylight and for your word which lights up our minds. We praise you for the earth, and all the people who live on it, and for our life which comes from you.

We know that you are good. You love us and do great things for us. So we all sing together:

Everyone: Holy, holy, holy Lord, God of power and might, heaven and earth are full of your glory.
Hosanna in the highest.

Priest: Father, you are always thinking about your people; you never forget us. You sent us your Son Jesus, who gave his life for us and who came to save us. He cured sick people; he cared for those who were poor and wept with those who were sad. He forgave sinners and taught us to forgive each other. He loved everyone and showed us how to be kind. He took children in his arms and blessed them. So we all sing together:

Everyone: Blessed is he who comes in the name of the Lord. Hosanna in the highest.

Priest: God our Father, all over the world your people praise you. So now we pray with the whole Church: with N., our pope, and N., our bishop. In heaven the blessed Virgin Mary, the apostles and all the saints always sing your praise. Now we join with them and with the angels to adore you as we sing:

Everyone: Holy, holy, holy Lord, God of power and might, heaven and earth are full of your glory.
Hosanna in the highest.
Blessed is he who comes in the name of the Lord.
Hosanna in the highest.

Priest: God our Father, you are most holy and we want to show you that we are grateful.

We bring you bread and wine and ask you to send your Holy Spirit to make these gifts the body and blood of Jesus your Son. Then we can offer to you what you have given to us.

On the night before he died, Jesus was having supper with his apostles. He took bread from the table. He gave you thanks and praise. Then he broke the bread, gave it to his friends, and said:

Take this, all of you, and eat it:
this is my body which will be given up for you.

The Eucharist

When supper was ended, Jesus took the cup that was filled with wine. He thanked you, gave it to his friends, and said:

> Take this, all of you, and drink from it:
> this is the cup of my blood,
> the blood of the new and everlasting covenant.
> It will be shed for you and for all
> so that sins may be forgiven.

Then he said to them:

> Do this in memory of me.

We do now what Jesus told us to do. We remember his death and his resurrection and we offer you, Father, the bread that gives us life, and the cup that saves us. Jesus brings us to you; welcome us as you welcome him.

Let us proclaim the mystery of faith:

Everyone: Christ has died, Christ is risen, Christ will come again.

Priest: Father, because you love us, you invite us to come to your table. Fill us with the joy of the Holy Spirit as we receive the body and blood of your Son.

Lord, you never forget any of your children. We ask you to take care of those we love, especially of N. and N.; and we pray for those who have died.

Remember everyone who is suffering from pain or sorrow. Remember Christians everywhere and all other people in the world.

We are filled with wonder and praise when we see what you do for us through Jesus your Son, and so we sing:

Through him, with him, in him, in the unity of the Holy Spirit, all glory and honour is yours, almighty Father, for ever and ever.

Everyone: Amen.
(Turn to page 24)

Eucharistic Prayer II

Priest: Father, it is our duty and our salvation, always and everywhere, to give you thanks through your beloved Son, Jesus Christ.

He is the Word through whom you made the universe, the Saviour you sent to redeem us. By the power of the Holy Spirit he took flesh and was born of the Virgin Mary. For our sake he opened his arms on the cross; he put an end to death and revealed the resurrection. In this he fulfilled your will and won for you a holy people.

And so we join the angels and the saints in proclaiming your glory as we say:

Everyone: Holy, holy, holy Lord, God of power and might, heaven and earth are full of your glory.
Hosanna in the highest.
Blessed is he who comes in the name of the Lord.
Hosanna in the highest.

Priest: Lord, you are holy indeed, the fountain of all holiness. Let your Spirit come upon these gifts to make them holy, so that they may become for us the body and blood of our Lord, Jesus Christ.

Before he was given up to death, a death he freely accepted, he took bread and gave you thanks. He broke the bread, gave it to his disciples, and said:

> Take this, all of you, and eat it:
> this is my body which will be given up for you.

21

When supper was ended, he took the cup. Again
he gave you thanks and praise, gave the cup to his
disciples, and said:

Take this, all of you, and drink from it:
this is the cup of my blood,
the blood of the new and everlasting covenant.
It will be shed for you and for all
so that sins may be forgiven.
Do this in memory of me.

Let us proclaim the mystery of faith:

Everyone: Christ has died, Christ is risen, Christ will come again.

Priest: In memory of his death and resurrection, we offer you,
Father, this life-giving bread, this saving cup. We thank
you for counting us worthy to stand in your presence
and serve you. May all of us who share in the body
and blood of Christ be brought together in unity by
the Holy Spirit.

Lord, remember your Church throughout the world;
make us grow in love, together with N., our pope, N.,
our bishop, and all the clergy.

Remember our brothers and sisters who have gone to
their rest in the hope of rising again; bring them and
all the departed into the light of your presence.

Have mercy on us all; make us worthy to share eternal
life with Mary, the virgin Mother of God, with the
apostles, and with all the saints who have done your
will throughout the ages. May we praise you in union
with them, and give you glory through your Son, Jesus
Christ.

Through him, with him, in him, in the unity of the
Holy Spirit, all glory and honour is yours, almighty
Father, for ever and ever.

Everyone: Amen.

What does it mean?

Covenant

When two people enter into a covenant agreement they promise to be faithful to one another. God entered into a covenant with us. He is our God, we are his People.

Forgiveness of sin

This is the forgiveness that comes from God, whose love is greater than our sins.

Do this in memory of me

Jesus asked the disciples to remember him by reliving what he said and did during the Last Supper.

The mystery of faith

Together we proclaim our belief in Christ who was born and died for us, rose to life, and will return one day.

Eternal life

This is life with God, which will be given to us fully after death.

Gestures

Extending the hands

When the priest extends his hands, he calls upon the Holy Spirit to consecrate the bread and wine, so that they become for us the body and blood of Christ.

Lifting the bread

The priest lifts the consecrated bread and then the chalice, so that the community may see and respectfully adore the body and blood of Christ.

Kneeling

This is a common way to show respect and to worship.

We say the Lord's Prayer

Jesus has taught us that God is the Father of all human beings and that we can call upon God at any time. Together we recite or sing this prayer.

Priest: Let us pray with confidence to the Father in the words our Saviour gave us:

Everyone: Our Father,
who art in heaven,
hallowed be thy name;
thy kingdom come;
thy will be done on earth
as it is in heaven.
Give us this day our daily bread;
and forgive us our trespasses
as we forgive those
who trespass against us;
and lead us not into temptation,
but deliver us from evil.

Priest: Deliver us, Lord, from every evil, and grant us peace in our day. In your mercy keep us free from sin and protect us from all anxiety as we wait in joyful hope for the coming of our Saviour, Jesus Christ.

Everyone: For the kingdom, the power and the glory are yours, now and forever.

What does it mean?

Saviour

This is one of the names we give to Jesus because he saves us from evil and death.

Heaven

Heaven is a special way of being with God after our life on earth is over.

Kingdom

Jesus speaks of God as king when he says: "The kingdom of God is at hand." With his life, Jesus shows us that God is present in our midst as a king who loves us. When we live as Jesus did, we welcome the kingdom of God.

Trespasses

These refer to our lack of love and to the sins we commit.

Temptation

This is a desire we sometimes feel to do things we know are wrong.

We share the peace of Christ

God is our Father and we are brothers and sisters in Christ.
In order to show that we are one family, the priest invites us to
offer each other a sign of peace.

Priest: Lord Jesus Christ, you said to your apostles:
I leave you peace, my peace I give you.
Look not on our sins, but on the faith of your Church,
and grant us the peace and unity of your kingdom
where you live for ever and ever.

Everyone: Amen.

Priest: The peace of the Lord be with you always.

Everyone: And also with you.

Priest: Let us offer each other a sign of peace.

*At this time, by a handshake, a kiss or a hug,
we give to those near us a sign of Christ's peace.
Immediately after, we say:*

Everyone: Lamb of God, you take away the sins of the world:
have mercy on us.

Lamb of God, you take away the sins of the world:
have mercy on us.

Lamb of God, you take away the sins of the world:
grant us peace.

What does it mean?

Unity

When we get together each Sunday to celebrate the Lord's Supper, we recognize our unity, or oneness, since we are all children of the same loving Father.

Lamb of God

In the Old Testament, believers offered a lamb to God. We call Jesus the Lamb of God because he offers his life to God.

Gestures

The sign of peace

We shake hands or hug one another to share the peace that comes from Christ. It is a sign of our commitment to live in peace with others.

We receive Jesus in communion

When we receive communion, the bread of life, we are fed with the life of Christ.

The priest breaks the host and says:

Priest: This is the Lamb of God who takes away the sins of the world. Happy are those who are called to his supper.

Everyone: Lord, I am not worthy to receive you, but only say the word and I shall be healed.

It is time to come up to receive communion. The priest or the communion minister says:

Priest: The body of Christ.

Everyone: Amen.

Why do we go to communion?

When we eat the bread and drink the wine, we receive Jesus. He gives himself to us this way so we can live for God. Sharing the body and blood of Christ in communion creates among us a special 'one-ness' with God and with each other.

Why is the bread we share during Mass called a "host"?

The word host means "victim who is offered." The consecrated host is Jesus Christ, who offers himself in order to give life to others.

The priest breaks the bread

The priest breaks the bread in the same way that Jesus did during the Last Supper, in order to share it. The early Christians used to call the Mass "the breaking of the bread."

Receiving the host

The priest or communion minister places the host in your open hand. You eat the bread carefully and return to your place. You take a few moments of quiet prayer to thank God for this bread of life.

The Lord sends us home

After announcements, the priest blesses us in the name of God. We are then sent to live out our faith among all the people we meet during the week.

Priest: The Lord be with you.

Everyone: And also with you.

Priest: May almighty God bless you, the Father, and the Son, and the Holy Spirit.

Everyone: Amen.

Then the priest sends us out, saying:

Priest: Go in peace to love and serve the Lord.

Everyone: Thanks be to God.

What does it mean?

The word "Mass"

The word "Mass" comes from the second word in the Latin phrase that was once used by the priest to announce the end of the Sunday celebration: *Ite missa est* – Go, the Mass is ended.

Communion for the sick

Sometimes people who are sick cannot be present at Sunday Mass. Certain members of the parish, known as communion ministers, can take consecrated hosts to the homes of sick people so that they can receive communion and be assured that the rest of the community is praying for them.

Gesture

Blessing

The priest makes the sign of the cross over the people in church. With this blessing they are sent out with the loving strength of God to live a life of love and service to others.

Dismissal

We cannot stay together in the church all week. When the Mass is ended, we must go our separate ways, in peace and love, to witness to the risen Jesus in the world today.

Liturgical Year

The readings for Sunday Mass and feast days change according to the liturgical calendar.

What is the liturgical year?

Throughout the year, Christians celebrate together important moments in Jesus' life. This is the liturgical year. There are five seasons: Advent, Christmas, Lent, Easter and Ordinary Time.

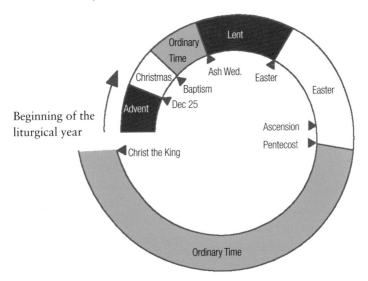

Beginning of the liturgical year

Advent is a time of waiting. It begins 4 weeks before Christmas. We prepare to welcome Jesus.

Christmas season celebrates the life of Jesus from his birth to his baptism. It includes Epiphany: Jesus welcomes the whole world.

During the 40 days of Lent—Ash Wednesday to Holy Saturday—we prepare for the great feast of Easter, the most important moment of the year.

Easter season is a time to celebrate Jesus' victory over death. It lasts from Easter Sunday to Pentecost, when the Holy Spirit comes upon the disciples.

The season in green above is called Ordinary Time because the Sundays are arranged using 'ordinal numbers.' It recounts many of the things Jesus did and said during his lifetime.

1st Sunday
of Advent

The word that Isaiah son of Amoz saw concerning Judah and Jerusalem. In days to come the mountain of the Lord's house shall be established as the highest of the mountains, and shall be raised above the hills; all the nations shall stream to it.

Many peoples shall come and say, "Come, let us go up to the mountain of the Lord, to the house of the God of Jacob; that he may teach us his ways and that we may walk in his paths."

For out of Zion shall go forth instruction, and the word of the Lord from Jerusalem. He shall judge between the nations, and shall arbitrate for many peoples; they shall beat their swords into ploughshares, and their spears into pruning hooks; nation shall not lift up sword against nation, neither shall they learn war any more.

O house of Jacob, come, let us walk in the light of the Lord!

The word of the Lord. **Thanks be to God.**

Psalm 122

R̥. **Let us go rejoicing to the house of the Lord.**

I was glad when they said to me,
"Let us go to the house of the Lord!"
Our feet are standing
within your gates, O Jerusalem. R̥.

To it the tribes go up, the tribes of the Lord,
as was decreed for Israel, to give thanks
to the name of the Lord.
For there the thrones for judgment were set up,
the thrones of the house of David. R̥.

Pray for the peace of Jerusalem:
"May they prosper who love you.
Peace be within your walls,
and security within your towers." R̥.

For the sake of my relatives and friends
I will say, "Peace be within you."
For the sake of the house of the Lord our God,
I will seek your good. R̥.

Brothers and sisters, you know what time it is, how it is now the moment for you to wake from sleep. For salvation is nearer to us now than when we became believers; the night is far gone, the day is near. Let us then lay aside the works of darkness and put on the armour of light; let us live honourably as in the day, not in revelling and drunkenness, not in debauchery and licentiousness, not in quarrelling and jealousy.

Instead, put on the Lord Jesus Christ, and make no provision for the flesh, to gratify its desires.

The word of the Lord. **Thanks be to God.**

Jesus spoke to his disciples: "As the days of Noah were, so will be the coming of the Son of Man. For as in those days before the flood they were eating and drinking, marrying and giving in marriage, until the day Noah entered the ark, and they knew nothing until the flood came and swept them all away, so too will be the coming of the Son of Man. Then two will be in the field; one will be taken and one will be left. Two women will be grinding meal together; one will be taken and one will be left.

"Keep awake, therefore, for you do not know on what day your Lord is coming. But understand this: if the owner of the house had known in what part of the night the thief was coming, he would have stayed awake and would not have let his house be broken into. Therefore you also must be ready, for the Son of Man is coming at an unexpected hour."

The Gospel of the Lord.
Praise to you, Lord Jesus Christ.

35

When the prophet Isaiah spoke of the mountain of the Lord's house, he was referring to the temple of Jerusalem. With this phrase he wanted to communicate that there will come a time when the God of Israel will be known and reverenced by all the people of the world.

Jacob was a grandson of Abraham and father of twelve sons, whom the twelve tribes of Israel were named after. So, the house of Jacob was a way to refer to all the people of Israel. Jacob died in Egypt, where his son Joseph grew to be a close friend and very important advisor to Pharaoh.

The works of darkness are bad actions that break our friendship with God and other people.

The armour of light is the willingness and desire to follow the teachings of Jesus. To be friends of Jesus we must be ready to struggle against all that might distance us from God.

Noah was the just man chosen by God to be saved from the flood, along with his family and two of every one of the animal species. God asked Noah to build a huge boat, called an ark, in which he, his family and the animals would live during the flood.

To keep awake is to avoid sleep throughout the night. But it also means being attentive so that nothing can surprise us. Christians must live in such a way that we're ready at any moment to meet our Lord.

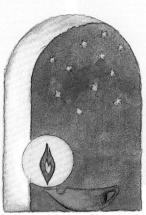

2nd Sunday of Advent

On that day:
A shoot shall come out from the stump of Jesse,
and a branch shall grow out of his roots.
The spirit of the Lord shall rest on him,
the spirit of wisdom and understanding,
the spirit of counsel and might,
the spirit of knowledge and the fear of the Lord.
His delight shall be in the fear of the Lord.

He shall not judge by what his eyes see,
or decide by what his ears hear;
but with righteousness he shall judge the poor,
and decide with equity for the meek of the earth;
he shall strike the earth with the rod of his mouth,
and with the breath of his lips he shall kill the wicked.
Righteousness shall be the belt around his waist,
and faithfulness the belt around his loins.

The wolf shall live with the lamb,
the leopard shall lie down with the kid,
the calf and the lion and the fatling together,
and a little child shall lead them.
The cow and the bear shall graze,
their young shall lie down together;
and the lion shall eat straw like the ox.
The nursing child shall play over the hole of the asp,
and the weaned child shall put its hand on the adder's den.
They will not hurt or destroy
on all my holy mountain;
for the earth will be full of the knowledge of the Lord
as the waters cover the sea.

On that day the root of Jesse shall stand
as a signal to the peoples;
the nations shall inquire of him,
and his dwelling shall be glorious.

The word of the Lord. **Thanks be to God.**

R. **In his days may righteousness flourish,
and peace abound forever.**

Give the king your justice, O God,
and your righteousness to a king's son.
May he judge your people with righteousness,
and your poor with justice. R.

In his days may righteousness flourish
and peace abound, until the moon is no more.
May he have dominion from sea to sea,
and from the River to the ends of the earth. R.

For he delivers the needy one who calls,
the poor and the one who has no helper.
He has pity on the weak and the needy,
and saves the lives of the needy. R.

May his name endure forever,
his fame continue as long as the sun.
May all nations be blessed in him;
may they pronounce him happy. R.

A reading from the Letter of Saint Paul to the Romans (15.4-9)

Brothers and sisters: Whatever was written in former days was written for our instruction, so that by steadfastness and by the encouragement of the Scriptures we might have hope.

May the God of steadfastness and encouragement grant you to live in harmony with one another, in accordance with Christ Jesus, so that together you may with one voice glorify the God and Father of our Lord Jesus Christ.

Welcome one another, therefore, just as Christ has welcomed you, for the glory of God. For I tell you that Christ has become a servant of the circumcised on behalf of the truth of God in order that he might confirm the promises given to the patriarchs, and in order that the Gentiles might glorify God for his mercy. As it is written, "Therefore I will confess you among the Gentiles, and sing praises to your name."

The word of the Lord. **Thanks be to God.**

In those days John the Baptist appeared in the wilderness of Judea, proclaiming, "Repent, for the kingdom of heaven has come near." This is the one of whom the Prophet Isaiah spoke when he said, "The voice of one crying out in the wilderness: 'Prepare the way of the Lord, make his paths straight.'"

Now John wore clothing of camel's hair with a leather belt around his waist, and his food was locusts and wild honey. Then the people of Jerusalem and all Judea were going out to him, and all the region along the Jordan, and they were baptized by him in the river Jordan, confessing their sins.

But when he saw many Pharisees and Sadducees coming for baptism, John said to them, "You brood of vipers! Who warned you to flee from the wrath to come? Bear fruit worthy of repentance. Do not presume to say to yourselves, 'We have Abraham as our father'; for I tell you, God is able from these stones to raise up children to Abraham. Even now the axe is lying at the root of the trees; every tree therefore that does not bear good fruit is cut down and thrown into the fire.

"I baptize you with water for repentance, but one who is more powerful than I is coming after me; I am not worthy to carry his sandals. He will baptize you with the Holy Spirit and fire. His winnowing fork is in his hand, and he will clear his threshing floor and will gather his wheat into the granary; but the chaff he will burn with unquenchable fire."

The Gospel of the Lord.
Praise to you, Lord Jesus Christ.

The prophet Isaiah was making a comparison between a branch that seemed withered and dead, and the hope of the people. When he referred to the appearance of a shoot that would give the tree life, he was referring to Jesus.

To have the spirit of fear of the Lord does not mean to be afraid of God. Rather, it signifies having a heart that is full of respect for the greatness of the Creator.

Hope is an attitude by which Christians live with the confidence that God will always support us. God made this promise in many ways, but especially when he sent us his son, Jesus Christ.

The patriarchs were the ancestors of the people of Israel. Abraham, Isaac and Jacob were all known by this name. They received the promise that the people would become a great nation.

John the Baptist was the son of Zechariah and Elizabeth, who was a cousin of the Virgin Mary. He was known as "the precursor" because he preached that the Messiah was about to arrive. He was called John the Baptist because those who were converted by his preaching were baptized in order to prepare themselves for the coming of the Saviour.

The Pharisees and the Sadducees were people who belonged to two Jewish religious sects. Pharisees were very strict and believed religion consisted in obeying the rules, forgetting that love is the greatest rule. The Sadducees believed themselves to be better than others, and did not believe in the resurrection.

When another person was recognized as being much more important than you, then you were not worthy to carry his sandals. That is because untying and carrying the sandals of a visitor was a job that slaves carried out.

3rd Sunday of Advent

The wilderness and the dry land shall be glad,
the desert shall rejoice and blossom;
like the crocus it shall blossom abundantly,
and rejoice with joy and singing.
The glory of Lebanon shall be given to it,
the majesty of Carmel and Sharon.
They shall see the glory of the Lord,
the majesty of our God.

Strengthen the weak hands,
and make firm the feeble knees.
Say to those who are of a fearful heart,
"Be strong, do not fear!
Here is your God.
He will come with vengeance,
with terrible recompense.
He will come and save you."

Then the eyes of the blind shall be opened,
and the ears of the deaf unstopped;
then the lame shall leap like a deer,
and the tongue of the mute sing for joy.

And the ransomed of the Lord shall return,
and come to Zion with singing;
everlasting joy shall be upon their heads;
they shall obtain joy and gladness,
and sorrow and sighing shall flee away.

The word of the Lord. **Thanks be to God.**

R̰ **Lord, come and save us.**

or **Alleluia!**

It is the Lord who keeps faith forever,
who executes justice for the oppressed;
who gives food to the hungry.
The Lord sets the prisoners free. R̰

The Lord opens the eyes of the blind
and lifts up those who are bowed down;
the Lord loves the righteous
and watches over the strangers. R̰

The Lord upholds the orphan and the widow,
but the way of the wicked he brings to ruin.
The Lord will reign forever,
your God, O Zion, for all generations. R̰

A reading from the Letter of Saint James (5.7-10)

Be patient, brothers and sisters, until the coming of the Lord. The farmer waits for the precious crop from the earth, being patient with it until it receives the early and the late rains. You also must be patient. Strengthen your hearts, for the coming of the Lord is near.

Brothers and sisters, do not grumble against one another, so that you may not be judged. See, the Judge is standing at the doors! As an example of suffering and patience, brothers and sisters, take the Prophets who spoke in the name of the Lord.

The word of the Lord. **Thanks be to God.**

When John the Baptist heard in prison about the deeds of the Christ, he sent word by his disciples who said to Jesus, "Are you the one who is to come, or are we to wait for another?"

Jesus answered them, "Go and tell John what you hear and see: the blind receive their sight, the lame walk, the lepers are cleansed, the deaf hear, the dead are raised, and the poor have good news brought to them. And blessed is anyone who takes no offence at me."

As they went away, Jesus began to speak to the crowds about John: "What did you go out into the wilderness to look at? A reed shaken by the wind? What then did you go out to see? Someone dressed in soft robes? Look, those who wear soft robes are in royal palaces. What then did you go out to see? A Prophet? Yes, I tell you, and more than a Prophet. This is the one about whom it is written, 'See, I am sending my messenger ahead of you, who will prepare your way before you.'

"Truly I tell you, among those born of women no one has arisen greater than John the Baptist; yet the least in the kingdom of heaven is greater than he."

The Gospel of the Lord. **Praise to you, Lord Jesus Christ.**

A crocus is among the first flowers that bloom in springtime.

Lebanon is a country at the eastern end of the Mediterranean Sea, bordering on modern-day Israel.

Carmel refers to a coastal mountain in Israel (see map, page 320). Mount Carmel marks the northern reach of the plain of Sharon, a flat region that includes the modern city of Tel Aviv.

The majesty of a king is his grandeur and power.

In the Old Testament there are many stories of battles and wars. Vengeance, which is a terrible thing, means getting even with someone by hitting them back after they have offended or hurt you. In this instance, the writer is trying to encourage the people to believe in God, who will eventually come to their aid.

If someone is oppressed then they are being very badly treated by others. Oppression deadens the soul and must be opposed by working for justice.

The coming of the Lord is a reference to the Second Coming of Jesus. The first Christians thought that Jesus would be returning to Earth in their own lifetimes, and so they understood this phrase in a very literal sense.

A reed is a thin shoot of a plant, often found near water.

Prophets were holy men and women who spoke publicly against poverty and injustice, and criticized the people whenever they refused to listen to God's word. Many of the books of the Old Testament were written by prophets (Isaiah, Jeremiah, Amos, and Micah, for example).

4th Sunday of Advent

The Lord spoke to Ahaz, saying, "Ask a sign of the Lord your God; let it be deep as Sheol or high as heaven." But Ahaz said, "I will not ask, and I will not put the Lord to the test."

Then Isaiah said: "Hear then, O house of David! Is it too little for you to weary the people, that you weary my God also? Therefore the Lord himself will give you a sign. Look, the young woman is with child and shall bear a son, and shall name him Emmanuel."

The word of the Lord. **Thanks be to God.**

Psalm 24

R. **May the Lord come in; he is king of glory.**

The earth is the Lord's and all that is in it,
the world, and those who live in it;
for he has founded it on the seas,
and established it on the rivers. R.

Who shall ascend the hill of the Lord?
And who shall stand in his holy place?
Someone who has clean hands and a pure heart,
who does not lift up their soul to what is false. R.

That person will receive blessing from the Lord,
and vindication from the God of their salvation.
Such is the company of those who seek him,
who seek the face of the God of Jacob. R.

A reading from the Letter of Saint Paul to the Romans (1.1-7)

From Paul, a servant of Jesus Christ, called to be an Apostle, set apart for the Gospel of God, which God promised beforehand through his Prophets in the holy Scriptures: the Gospel concerning his Son, who was descended from David according to the flesh and was declared to be Son of God with power according to the spirit of holiness by resurrection from the dead, Jesus Christ our Lord.

Through Christ we have received grace and apostleship to bring about the obedience of faith among all the Gentiles for the sake of his name, including yourselves who are called to belong to Jesus Christ.

To all God's beloved in Rome, who are called to be saints: Grace to you and peace from God our Father and the Lord Jesus Christ.

The word of the Lord. **Thanks be to God.**

A reading from the holy Gospel according to Matthew (1.18-24)

The birth of Jesus the Christ took place in this way. When his mother Mary had been engaged to Joseph, but before they lived together, she was found to be with child from the Holy Spirit. Her husband Joseph, being a righteous man and unwilling to expose her to public disgrace, planned to dismiss her quietly.

But just when he had resolved to do this, an Angel of the Lord appeared to him in a dream and said, "Joseph, son of David, do not be afraid to take Mary as your wife, for the child conceived in her is from the Holy Spirit. She will bear a son, and you are to name him Jesus, for he will save his people from their sins."

All this took place to fulfill what had been spoken by the Lord through the Prophet: "Look, the virgin shall conceive and bear a son, and they shall name him Emmanuel," which means, "God is with us." When Joseph awoke from sleep, he did as the Angel of the Lord commanded him; he took her as his wife.

The Gospel of the Lord. **Praise to you, Lord Jesus Christ.**

KEY WORDS

Ahaz was a king of Israel who was not well thought of. He was not true to the covenant with the Lord: he worshipped other gods that he himself had created and he closed the temple.

When the prophet Isaiah spoke to the house of David, he was speaking to all the Israelites. This was the name by which all the people of Israel were known.

The Letter of Paul to the Romans was the longest letter that Saint Paul wrote. The Christians who lived in Rome belonged to a small community. Paul wanted to travel to preach in Spain, and stop on the way in Rome to visit the Christians. He sent them this letter in order to introduce himself, to encourage them, and to remind them of the teachings of Jesus.

The word Gospel means the whole message that Jesus brought us. It is a word meaning the "Good News."

Apostleship is a mission that God gave to Saint Paul, to announce the Good News of the resurrection of Jesus. This is also the mission of all Christians.

The Gentiles are people who are not Jewish.

Saint Matthew was the author of one of the four gospels. This story clearly tells us about the life of Jesus. It emphasizes that he is the promised Messiah, and that the Church is now the Chosen People, the new Israel.

Joseph and Mary were engaged, but they did not live together before marriage. For this reason Joseph was surprised that Mary was expecting a baby.

Christmas
The Nativity of the Lord

ADELA GENINA

The people who walked in darkness have seen a great light;
those who lived in a land of deep darkness—
on them light has shone.
You have multiplied the nation,
you have increased its joy;
they rejoice before you
as with joy at the harvest,
as people exult when dividing plunder.

For the yoke of their burden,
and the bar across their shoulders,
the rod of their oppressor,
you have broken as on the day of Midian.

For a child has been born for us,
a son given to us;
authority rests upon his shoulders;
and he is named
Wonderful Counsellor, Mighty God,
Everlasting Father, Prince of Peace.

His authority shall grow continually,
and there shall be endless peace
for the throne of David and his kingdom.
He will establish and uphold it
with justice and with righteousness
from this time onward and forevermore.
The zeal of the Lord of hosts will do this.

The word of the Lord. **Thanks be to God.**

R. **Today is born our Saviour, Christ the Lord.**

O sing to the Lord a new song;
sing to the Lord, all the earth.
Sing to the Lord, bless his name;
tell of his salvation from day to day. R.

Declare his glory among the nations,
his marvellous works among all the peoples.
For great is the Lord, and greatly to be praised;
he is to be revered above all gods. R.

Let the heavens be glad, and let the earth rejoice;
let the sea roar, and all that fills it;
let the field exult, and everything in it.
Then shall all the trees of the forest sing for joy. R.

Rejoice before the Lord; for he is coming,
for he is coming to judge the earth.
He will judge the world with righteousness,
and the peoples with his truth. R.

A reading from the Letter of Saint Paul to Titus
(2.11-14)

Beloved: The grace of God has appeared, bringing salvation to all, training us to renounce impiety and worldly passions, and in the present age to live lives that are self-controlled, upright, and godly, while we wait for the blessed hope and the manifestation of the glory of our great God and Saviour, Jesus Christ.

He it is who gave himself for us that he might redeem us from all iniquity and purify for himself a people of his own who are zealous for good deeds.

The word of the Lord. **Thanks be to God.**

In those days a decree went out from Caesar Augustus that all the world should be registered. This was the first registration and was taken while Quirinius was governor of Syria. All went to their own towns to be registered. Joseph also went from the town of Nazareth in Galilee to Judea, to the city of David called Bethlehem, because he was descended from the house and family of David. He went to be registered with Mary, to whom he was engaged and who was expecting a child.

While they were there, the time came for her to deliver her child. And she gave birth to her firstborn son and wrapped him in swaddling clothes, and laid him in a manger, because there was no place for them in the inn.

In that region there were shepherds living in the fields, keeping watch over their flock by night. Then an Angel of the Lord stood before them, and the glory of the Lord shone around them, and they were terrified. But the Angel said to them, "Do not be afraid; for see—I am bringing you good news of great joy for all the people: to you is born this day in the city of David a Saviour, who is the Christ, the Lord. This will be a sign for you: you will find a child wrapped in swaddling clothes and lying in a manger."

And suddenly there was with the Angel a multitude of the heavenly host, praising God and saying, "Glory to God in the highest heaven, and on earth peace among those whom he favours!"

When the Angels had left them and gone into heaven, the shepherds said to one another, "Let us go now to Bethlehem and see this thing that has taken place, which the Lord has made known to us." So they went with haste and found Mary and Joseph, and the child lying in the manger.

The Gospel of the Lord.
Praise to you, Lord Jesus Christ.

To exult is to be extremely happy.

A yoke is a heavy harness, usually made of wood, which ties oxen to a plough. Wearing such a thing would be awkward and uncomfortable. The coming of Jesus is thus compared to the lifting of a great burden from a suffering humanity.

To be revered is to be held in the highest esteem. We revere God because he loves us and does mighty things for us.

Grace is the action of the Spirit in the lives of people and in God's creation. By the gift of grace we become better followers of Jesus.

When we renounce something we reject it or turn our backs on it. Thus, God asks us to renounce sinful behaviour.

A decree was an order from the Roman ruler of that time. It had to be obeyed.

Syria is a country in the Middle East, which borders Israel and Lebanon. In the time of Jesus, the ruler of Syria was responsible for this entire region.

A manger is a wooden crate where hay is placed to feed the animals in a stable. The baby Jesus was placed in a manger soon after he was born. This was an amazing thing: that God would choose to be born in such a stark and humble manner.

Glory to God in the highest and on earth peace to all people!

Merry Christmas!

December 26

Holy Family

The Lord honours a father above his children,
and he confirms a mother's rights over her sons.
Whoever honours their father atones for sins
and gains preservation from them;
when they pray, they will be heard.
Whoever respects their mother
is like one who lays up treasure.
The person who honours their father
will have joy in their own children,
and when they pray they will be heard.
Whoever respects their father will have a long life,
and whoever honours their mother obeys the Lord.

My child, help your father in his old age,
and do not grieve him as long as he lives.
Even if his mind fails, be patient with him;
because you have all your faculties,
do not despise him all the days of his life.
For kindness to your father will not be forgotten,
and will be credited to you against your sins—
a house raised in justice for you.

The word of the Lord. **Thanks be to God.**

Psalm 128

R. **Blessed is everyone who fears the Lord.**

or **Blessed is everyone who fears the Lord, who walks in his ways.**

Blessed is everyone who fears the Lord,
who walks in his ways.
You shall eat the fruit of the labour of your hands;
you shall be happy, and it shall go well with you. R.

Your wife will be like a fruitful vine
within your house;
your children will be like olive shoots
around your table. R.

Thus shall the man be blessed who fears the Lord.
The Lord bless you from Zion.
May you see the prosperity of Jerusalem
all the days of your life. R.

The shorter reading ends at the asterisks.

Brothers and sisters: As God's chosen ones, holy and beloved, clothe yourselves with compassion, kindness, humility, meekness, and patience. Bear with one another and, if anyone has a complaint against another, forgive each other; just as the Lord has forgiven you, so you also must forgive. Above all, clothe yourselves with love, which binds everything together in perfect harmony. And let the peace of Christ rule in your hearts, to which indeed you were called in the one body. And be thankful.

Let the word of Christ dwell in you richly; teach and admonish one another in all wisdom; and with gratitude in your hearts sing Psalms, hymns, and spiritual songs to God. And whatever you do, in word or deed, do everything in the name of the Lord Jesus, giving thanks to God the Father through him.

* * *

Wives, be subject to your husbands, as is fitting in the Lord. Husbands, love your wives and never treat them harshly. Children, obey your parents in everything, for this is your acceptable duty in the Lord. Fathers, do not provoke your children, or they may lose heart.

The word of the Lord. **Thanks be to God.**

After the wise men had left, an Angel of the Lord appeared to Joseph in a dream and said, "Get up, take the child and his mother, and flee to Egypt, and remain there until I tell you; for Herod is about to search for the child, to destroy him." Then Joseph got up, took the child and his mother by night, and went to Egypt, and remained there until the death of Herod. This was to fulfill what had been spoken by the Lord through the Prophet, "Out of Egypt I have called my son."

When Herod died, an Angel of the Lord suddenly appeared in a dream to Joseph in Egypt and said, "Get up, take the child and his mother, and go to the land of Israel, for those who were seeking the child's life are dead." Then Joseph got up, took the child and his mother, and went to the land of Israel.

But when he heard that Archelaus was ruling over Judea in place of his father Herod, he was afraid to go there. And after being warned in a dream, he went away to the district of Galilee. There he made his home in a town called Nazareth, so that what had been spoken through the Prophets might be fulfilled, "He will be called a Nazorean."

The Gospel of the Lord. **Praise to you, Lord Jesus Christ.**

In the Bible the phrase "obey the Lord" is not used to make us fear God. How could we fear such a wonderful parent? Obey the Lord means to recognize how great God is, how good, how very important, and that we should show tenderness and respect to God.

A vine is a plant that gives grapes. A fruitful vine gives many grapes. In biblical times, a woman was considered blessed by God when she had children.

Someone who is holy is set apart for God's service. All of us Christians are chosen by God since the time of our baptism, when we were united with Jesus.

Giving thanks to God is a task for all Christians. Gratitude is a virtue, best expressed when we show compassion for others and try to be of assistance to those who are suffering.

The wise men were scholars who came from the East because they had discovered the birth of the Messiah was about to take place. They were likely people who dedicated themselves to studying the stars.

This is a reference to Herod the Great, a friend of the Romans. He came to govern many lands. He was known both for his cruelty as well as for his lack of interest in religion. His son Herod Antipas was the man who was in Jerusalem on the day that they crucified Jesus.

Solemnity of Mary,
the Holy Mother of God

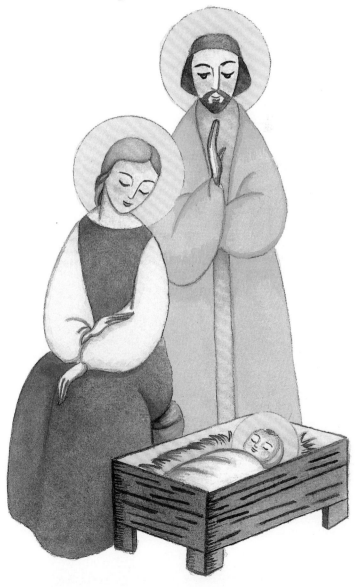

A reading from the book of Numbers (6.22-27)

The Lord spoke to Moses: Speak to Aaron and his sons, saying,
Thus you shall bless the children of Israel: You shall say to them,

The Lord bless you and keep you;
the Lord make his face to shine upon you,
and be gracious to you;
the Lord lift up his countenance upon you,
and give you peace.

So they shall put my name on the children of Israel, and I will
bless them.

The word of the Lord. **Thanks be to God.**

Psalm 67

R̲ **May God be gracious to us and bless us.**

May God be gracious to us and bless us
and make his face to shine upon us,
that your way may be known upon earth,
your saving power among all nations. R̲

Let the nations be glad and sing for joy,
for you judge the peoples with equity
and guide the nations upon earth.
Let the peoples praise you, O God;
let all the peoples praise you. R̲

The earth has yielded its increase;
God, our God, has blessed us.
May God continue to bless us;
let all the ends of the earth revere him. R̲

A reading from the Letter of Saint Paul to the Galatians (4.4-7)

Brothers and sisters: When the fullness of time had come, God sent his Son, born of a woman, born under the law, in order to redeem those who were under the law, so that we might receive adoption to sonship.

And because you are sons and daughters, God has sent the Spirit of his Son into our hearts, crying, "Abba! Father!" So you are no longer slave but son, and if son then also heir, through God.

The word of the Lord. **Thanks be to God.**

A reading from the holy Gospel according to Luke (2.16-21)

The shepherds went with haste to Bethlehem and found Mary and Joseph, and the child lying in the manger. When they saw this, they made known what had been told them about this child; and all who heard it were amazed at what the shepherds told them.

But Mary treasured all these words and pondered them in her heart.

The shepherds returned, glorifying and praising God for all they had heard and seen, as it had been told them.

After eight days had passed, it was time to circumcise the child; and he was called Jesus, the name given by the Angel before he was conceived in the womb.

The Gospel of the Lord.
Praise to you, Lord Jesus Christ.

The book of Numbers is part of the Bible. It is called 'Numbers' because it talks about many numbers and times when the people of Israel were counted. In Hebrew, it is called "In the Desert," because it tells of the travels of the Israelites, after they left slavery in Egypt.

Moses was a friend of God who was born in Egypt when the Israelites were slaves there. When God asked him to lead the people to freedom, Moses said yes because he loved God and didn't want the people to suffer any more. The people left Egypt on a journey called the 'Exodus' about 1,250 years before the time of Jesus.

Aaron, Moses' older brother, helped him free the Israelites. When Moses went up Mount Sinai to receive God's law, Aaron stayed with the people.

Children of Israel is the name of the people God chose to help everyone in the world know God's love.

To judge with equity is to be fair to everyone. In the psalm, the psalmist is praising God for God's fairness to all people on earth.

Fullness of time means when the time was right for God to send Jesus into the world.

In Aramaic, the language Jesus spoke, Abba means 'Daddy.' By calling God "Abba," Jesus shows that we can talk to God with the same trust and love that small children have for their father.

A manger is the place in a barn or stable for the animals' food. Its name is from the French word *manger*, to eat.

To ponder means to think about something a lot. Like all mothers, Mary remembered all the details surrounding the birth of her child.

Epiphany of the Lord

Arise, shine, for your light has come,
and the glory of the Lord has risen upon you!
For darkness shall cover the earth,
and thick darkness the peoples;
but the Lord will arise upon you,
and his glory will appear over you.
Nations shall come to your light,
and kings to the brightness of your dawn.
Lift up your eyes and look around;
they all gather together, they come to you;
your sons shall come from far away,
and your daughters shall be carried on their nurses' arms.

Then you shall see and be radiant;
your heart shall thrill and rejoice,
because the abundance of the sea shall be brought to you,
the wealth of the nations shall come to you.
A multitude of camels shall cover you,
the young camels of Midian and Ephah;
all those from Sheba shall come.
They shall bring gold and frankincense,
and shall proclaim the praise of the Lord.

The word of the Lord.
Thanks be to God.

R. **Lord, every nation on earth will adore you.**

Give the king your justice, O God,
and your righteousness to a king's son.
May he judge your people with righteousness,
and your poor with justice. R.

In his days may righteousness flourish
and peace abound, until the moon is no more.
May he have dominion from sea to sea,
and from the River to the ends of the earth. R.

May the kings of Tarshish and of the isles
render him tribute,
may the kings of Sheba and Seba bring gifts.
May all kings fall down before him,
all nations give him service. R.

For he delivers the needy one who calls,
the poor and the one who has no helper.
He has pity on the weak and the needy,
and saves the lives of the needy. R.

A reading from the Letter of Saint Paul to the Ephesians (3.2-3, 5-6)

Brothers and sisters: Surely you have already heard of the commission of God's grace that was given me for you, and how the mystery was made known to me by revelation.

In former generations this mystery was not made known to humankind as it has now been revealed to his holy Apostles and Prophets by the Spirit: that is, the Gentiles have become fellow heirs, members of the same body, and sharers in the promise in Christ Jesus through the Gospel.

The word of the Lord. **Thanks be to God.**

In the time of King Herod, after Jesus was born in Bethlehem of Judea, wise men from the East came to Jerusalem, asking, "Where is the child who has been born king of the Jews? For we observed his star at its rising, and have come to pay him homage."

When King Herod heard this, he was frightened, and all Jerusalem with him; and calling together all the chief priests and scribes of the people, he inquired of them where the Messiah was to be born. They told him, "In Bethlehem of Judea; for so it has been written by the Prophet: 'And you, Bethlehem, in the land of Judah, are by no means least among the rulers of Judah; for from you shall come a ruler who is to shepherd my people Israel.'"

Then Herod secretly called for the wise men and learned from them the exact time when the star had appeared. Then he sent them to Bethlehem, saying, "Go and search diligently for the child; and when you have found him, bring me word so that I may also go and pay him homage."

When they had heard the king, they set out; and there, ahead of them, went the star that they had seen at its rising, until it stopped over the place where the child was. When they saw that the star had stopped, they were overwhelmed with joy.

On entering the house, they saw the child with Mary his mother; and they knelt down and paid him homage. Then, opening their treasure chests, they offered him gifts of gold, frankincense, and myrrh.

And having been warned in a dream not to return to Herod, they left for their own country by another road.

The Gospel of the Lord.
Praise to you, Lord Jesus Christ.

Epiphany is a Greek word that means 'unveiling,' where something is revealed. God revealed his love for all people by sending us his Son, Jesus, as a baby.

Midian, Ephah and Sheba were three ancient kingdoms near Israel. In the book of the prophet Isaiah in the Bible, they represent all the nations outside Israel.

The Ephesians were a group of Christians in the city of Ephesus. A letter Paul wrote to them is now part of the Bible. Ephesus is located in modern-day Turkey, near the town of Selçuk.

To know something by revelation means that God has shown or given someone this knowledge.

A mystery is something that is very hard to understand. In Paul's letter to the Ephesians, it means God's plan to create a human community in Christ.

Bethlehem of Judea is the city of King David, one of Jesus' ancestors. Joseph and Mary went to Bethlehem for a census (an official counting of all the people). Jesus was born during their stay there. See the map on page 320.

To pay someone homage is to show your respect or honour for them in a public way, such as by bowing or bringing gifts.

Messiah is an Aramaic word meaning 'anointed'. The chosen person was blessed with holy oil and given a special mission. The Greek word for 'anointed' is 'Christ.'

Gold, frankincense and myrrh were three very expensive gifts: gold is a precious metal; frankincense and myrrh are rare, sweet-smelling incenses. Myrrh is the main ingredient in holy anointing oil.

Baptism of the Lord

GENINA

Thus says the Lord:
"Here is my servant, whom I uphold,
my chosen, in whom my soul delights;
I have put my spirit upon him;
he will bring forth justice to the nations.
He will not cry or lift up his voice,
or make it heard in the street;
a bruised reed he will not break,
and a dimly burning wick he will not quench;
he will faithfully bring forth justice.
He will not grow faint or be crushed
until he has established justice in the earth;
and the coastlands wait for his teaching.

"I am the Lord, I have called you in righteousness,
I have taken you by the hand and kept you;
I have given you as a covenant to the people,
a light to the nations,
to open the eyes that are blind,
to bring out the prisoners from the dungeon,
from the prison those who sit in darkness."

The word of the Lord. **Thanks be to God.**

Psalm 29

R. **The Lord will bless his people with peace.**

Ascribe to the Lord, O heavenly beings,
ascribe to the Lord glory and strength.
Ascribe to the Lord the glory of his name;
worship the Lord in holy splendour. R.

The voice of the Lord is over the waters;
the Lord, over mighty waters.
The voice of the Lord is powerful;
the voice of the Lord is full of majesty. R.

The God of glory thunders,
and in his temple all say, "Glory!"
The Lord sits enthroned over the flood;
the Lord sits enthroned as king forever. R.

Peter began to speak:

"I truly understand that God shows no partiality, but in every nation anyone who fears him and does what is right is acceptable to him. You know the message he sent to the people of Israel, preaching peace by Jesus Christ—he is Lord of all. That message spread throughout Judea, beginning in Galilee after the baptism that John announced: how God anointed Jesus of Nazareth with the Holy Spirit and with power; how he went about doing good and healing all who were oppressed by the devil, for God was with him."

The word of the Lord. **Thanks be to God.**

A reading from the holy Gospel according to Matthew (3.13-17)

Jesus came from Galilee to John at the Jordan, to be baptized by him. John would have prevented him, saying, "I need to be baptized by you, and do you come to me?" But Jesus answered him, "Let it be so for now; for it is proper for us in this way to fulfill all righteousness." Then John consented.

And when Jesus had been baptized, just as he came up from the water, suddenly the heavens were opened to him and he saw the Spirit of God descending like a dove and alighting on him. And a voice from heaven said, "This is my Son, the Beloved, with whom I am well pleased."

The Gospel of the Lord.
Praise to you, Lord Jesus Christ.

Isaiah was a friend of God who lived about 800 years before Jesus. God chose him to help the people of Israel turn back to God.

Servant, or a person who serves others, describes someone who does God's will. In the book of Isaiah, the Lord's servant is a chosen one who suffers in order to bring forth justice. Christians believe this person is Jesus.

God's servant will not rest until he has established justice. We are called to this work as well, by following God's commandment to love God and our neighbour.

The Acts of the Apostles is a book in the Bible that describes how the Church grew after Jesus rose from the dead. Written by Luke, who also wrote a gospel, it mostly tells the story of Peter and Paul.

When Peter showed that he had great faith in Jesus, Jesus chose him to be the leader of the apostles. In today's reading from the Acts of the Apostles, Peter speaks as the head of the new community.

To show partiality is to be nice to one person and not to another. God is impartial and treats everyone the same way: with love.

The baptism that John announced called people to turn back to God. John the Baptist baptized people in the River Jordan to show that their sins were washed away. Today, the sacrament of baptism unites us with Jesus and makes us part of the Church.

2nd Sunday in Ordinary Time

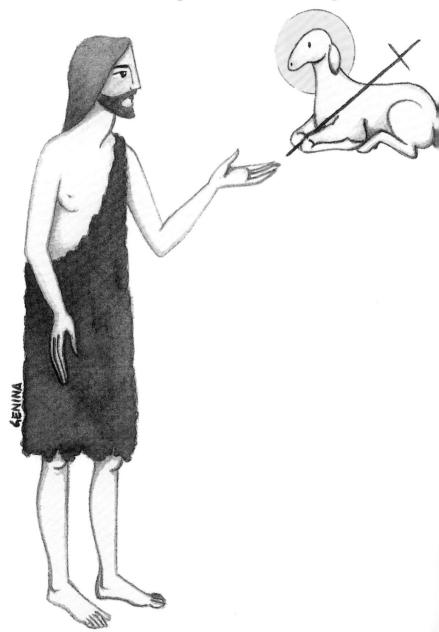

The Lord said to me,
"You are my servant, Israel, in whom I will be glorified."

And now the Lord says,
who formed me in the womb to be his servant,
to bring Jacob back to him,
and that Israel might be gathered to him,
for I am honoured in the sight of the Lord,
and my God has become my strength.

He says,
"It is too small a thing that you should be my servant
to raise up the tribes of Jacob
and to restore the survivors of Israel;
I will give you as a light to the nations,
that my salvation may reach to the end of the earth."

The word of the Lord. **Thanks be to God.**

Psalm 40

R. **Here I am, Lord; I come to do your will.**

I waited patiently for the Lord;
he inclined to me and heard my cry.
He put a new song in my mouth,
a song of praise to our God. R.

Sacrifice and offering you do not desire,
but you have given me an open ear.
Burnt offering and sin offering
you have not required. R.

Then I said, "Here I am;
in the scroll of the book it is written of me.
I delight to do your will, O my God;
your law is within my heart." R.

I have told the glad news of deliverance
in the great congregation;
see, I have not restrained my lips,
as you know, O Lord. R.

A reading from the first Letter of Saint Paul to the Corinthians (1.1-3)

From Paul, called to be an Apostle of Christ Jesus by the will of God, and from our brother Sosthenes. To the Church of God that is in Corinth, to those who are sanctified in Christ Jesus, called to be saints, together with all those who in every place call on the name of our Lord Jesus Christ, both their Lord and ours:

Grace to you and peace from God our Father and the Lord Jesus Christ.

The word of the Lord. **Thanks be to God.**

A reading from the holy Gospel according to John (1.29-34)

John the Baptist saw Jesus coming toward him and declared, "Here is the Lamb of God who takes away the sin of the world! This is he of whom I said, 'After me comes a man who ranks ahead of me because he was before me.' I myself did not know him; but I came baptizing with water for this reason, that he might be revealed to Israel."

And John testified, "I saw the Spirit descending from heaven like a dove, and remain on him. I myself did not know him, but the one who sent me to baptize with water said to me, 'He on whom you see the Spirit descend and remain is the one who baptizes with the Holy Spirit.' And I myself have seen and have testified that this is the Son of God."

The Gospel of the Lord. **Praise to you, Lord Jesus Christ.**

Jacob was the grandson of Abraham and the father of many children. His children were the first people in the twelve tribes of the Jewish people. In this reading, Jacob represents all the people of Israel.

God's servant will bring together the tribes of Israel. Christians believe that Jesus, the Messiah, came to bring all people back to God. God's servant is a light to all the nations.

Sosthenes was a friend and companion of Paul who helped him spread the Good News of Jesus Christ to the Corinthians.

When Paul wishes "grace to you and peace," he is expressing his wish that we will all live according to the gifts that Jesus' salvation brings.

The Lamb of God is Jesus. Jewish people made sacrifices of animals to God. Because Jesus' sacrifice brought us back to God, John the Baptist compares Jesus to a lamb.

To testify is to announce a truth with words and deeds. We testify that Jesus lives when we live as he taught us.

John the Baptist called Jesus the Son of God, showing that Jesus is the Messiah, the long-awaited one sent from God to bring us salvation.

3rd Sunday in Ordinary Time

There will be no gloom for those who were in anguish. In the former time the Lord brought into contempt the land of Zebulun and the land of Naphtali, but in the latter time he will make glorious the way of the sea, the land beyond the Jordan, Galilee of the nations.

The people who walked in darkness have seen a great light; those who lived in a land of deep darkness—on them light has shone. You have multiplied the nation, you have increased its joy; they rejoice before you as with joy at the harvest, as people exult when dividing plunder.

For the yoke of their burden, and the bar across their shoulders, the rod of their oppressor, you have broken as on the day of Midian.

The word of the Lord. **Thanks be to God.**

Psalm 27

R. **The Lord is my light and my salvation.**

The Lord is my light and my salvation;
whom shall I fear?
The Lord is the stronghold of my life;
of whom shall I be afraid? R.

One thing I asked of the Lord, that will I seek after:
to live in the house of the Lord all the days of my life,
to behold the beauty of the Lord,
and to inquire in his temple. R.

I believe that I shall see the goodness of the Lord
in the land of the living.
Wait for the Lord; be strong,
and let your heart take courage; wait for the Lord! R.

I appeal to you, brothers and sisters, by the name of our Lord Jesus Christ, that all of you be in agreement and that there be no divisions among you, but that you be united in the same mind and the same purpose.

For it has been reported to me by Chloe's people that there are quarrels among you, my brothers and sisters. What I mean is that each of you says, "I belong to Paul," or "I belong to Apollos," or "I belong to Cephas," or "I belong to Christ."

Has Christ been divided? Was Paul crucified for you? Or were you baptized in the name of Paul?

For Christ did not send me to baptize but to proclaim the Gospel, and not with eloquent wisdom so that the Cross of Christ might not be emptied of its power.

For the message about the Cross is foolishness to those who are perishing, but to us who are being saved it is the power of God.

The word of the Lord. **Thanks be to God.**

A reading from the holy Gospel according to Matthew (4.12-23)

The shorter version ends at the asterisks.

When Jesus heard that John had been arrested, he withdrew to Galilee. He left Nazareth and made his home in Capernaum by the sea, in the territory of Zebulun and Naphtali, so that what had been spoken through the Prophet Isaiah might be fulfilled: "Land of Zebulun, land of Naphtali, on the road by the sea, across the Jordan, Galilee of the Gentiles—the people who sat in darkness have seen a great light, and for those who sat in the region and shadow of death light has dawned."

From that time Jesus began to proclaim, "Repent, for the kingdom of heaven has come near."

* * *

As he walked by the Sea of Galilee, he saw two brothers, Simon, who is called Peter, and Andrew his brother, casting a net into the sea, for they were fishermen. And he said to them, "Come, follow me, and I will make you fishers of people." Immediately they left their nets and followed him.

As he went from there, he saw two other brothers, James son of Zebedee and his brother John, in the boat with their father Zebedee, mending their nets, and he called them. Immediately they left the boat and their father, and followed him.

Jesus went throughout Galilee, teaching in their synagogues and proclaiming the good news of the kingdom and curing every disease and every sickness among the people.

The Gospel of the Lord. **Praise to you, Lord Jesus Christ.**

When Isaiah mentions Zebulun and Naphtali, his listeners remember towns where God had shown his anger because the people did not heed his words. God promises to send the Messiah who will bring freedom and joy to God's people.

People, families or even nations can walk in darkness when they feel lost and do not know where to turn. They need God's light to show them the way.

Saul was a man who bullied and terrorized the first Christians. One day, he had a vision of the risen Jesus and the experience changed his whole life. When he was baptized he changed his name to Paul and became a great apostle, travelling to cities all around the Mediterranean Sea to tell people about the love of Jesus. Several letters he wrote are now in the Bible.

The holy Gospel according to Matthew is the first book in the New Testament. This gospel tells us about the life of Jesus. It points out that he is the promised Messiah, and that the Church is the chosen people, the new Israel.

To repent means to be sorry for doing something wrong, and to change your way of thinking and live for the better.

In the kingdom of heaven, all people will be brought together in God. We will all live like brothers and sisters, sharing in God's abundant love and mercy.

January 30

4th Sunday
in Ordinary Time

Seek the Lord, all you humble of the land,
who do his commands;
seek righteousness, seek humility;
perhaps you may be hidden on the day of the Lord's wrath.

For I will leave in the midst of you
a people humble and lowly.
They shall seek refuge in the name of the Lord—
the remnant of Israel;
they shall do no wrong and utter no lies,
nor shall a deceitful tongue be found in their mouths.
Then they will pasture and lie down,
and no one shall make them afraid.

The word of the Lord. **Thanks be to God.**

Psalm 146

R̥. **Blessed are the poor in spirit;
the kingdom of heaven is theirs!**

or **Alleluia!**

It is the Lord who keeps faith forever,
who executes justice for the oppressed;
who gives food to the hungry.
The Lord sets the prisoners free. R̥.

The Lord opens the eyes of the blind
and lifts up those who are bowed down;
the Lord loves the righteous
and watches over the strangers. R̥.

The Lord upholds the orphan and the widow,
but the way of the wicked he brings to ruin.
The Lord will reign forever,
your God, O Zion, for all generations. R̥.

A reading from the first Letter of Saint Paul to the Corinthians (1.26-31)

Consider your own call, brothers and sisters: not many of you were wise by human standards, not many were powerful, not many were of noble birth. But God chose what is foolish in the world to shame the wise; God chose what is weak in the world to shame the strong; God chose what is low and despised in the world, things that are not, to reduce to nothing things that are, so that no one might boast in the presence of God.

God is the source of your life in Christ Jesus, who became for us wisdom from God, and righteousness and sanctification and redemption, in order that, as it is written, "Let the one who boasts, boast in the Lord."

The word of the Lord. **Thanks be to God.**

A reading from the holy Gospel according to Matthew (5.1-12)

When Jesus saw the crowds, he went up the mountain; and after he sat down, his disciples came to him. Then he began to speak, and taught them, saying:

"Blessed are the poor in spirit,
    for theirs is the kingdom of heaven.
Blessed are those who mourn, for they will be comforted.
Blessed are the meek, for they will inherit the earth.
Blessed are those who hunger and thirst for righteousness,
    for they will be filled.

"Blessed are the merciful, for they will receive mercy.
Blessed are the pure in heart, for they will see God.
Blessed are the peacemakers,
    for they will be called children of God.
Blessed are those who are persecuted for righteousness' sake,
    for theirs is the kingdom of heaven.

"Blessed are you when people revile you and persecute you and utter all kinds of evil against you falsely on my account. Rejoice and be glad, for your reward is great in heaven, for in the same way they persecuted the Prophets who were before you."

The Gospel of the Lord. **Praise to you, Lord Jesus Christ.**

The prophet Zephaniah lived about 700 years before Jesus was born. The people of Israel had fallen away from their faith. Zephaniah tried to help them return to God.

People who are humble do not show off or boast. They don't worry about how much money they have, but try in their hearts to do the will of God.

In times when many of the Israelites had turned away from God, the few who remained faithful to God's covenant were call the remnant of Israel.

The Corinthians were a community of Christians who lived in Corinth, a city in Greece. Paul wrote them several letters, two of which are in the Bible.

The source is the spot where a river or a stream begins —where life-giving water originates. We are united with Jesus by the waters of baptism.

The poor in spirit are people who put their confidence in God and do not worry about material things. The poor in spirit are in fact rich in God's spirit.

Those who are merciful share in God's loving concern for everyone, but most especially for the poor and the weak. Jesus asks us to be merciful.

February 6

5th Sunday in Ordinary Time

GENINA

Thus says the Lord:
Is this not the fast that I choose:
to loose the bonds of injustice,
to undo the thongs of the yoke,
to let the oppressed go free,
and to break every yoke?
Is it not to share your bread with the hungry,
and bring the homeless poor into your house;
when you see the naked, to cover them,
and not to hide yourself from your own kin?

Then your light shall break forth like the dawn,
and your healing shall spring up quickly;
your vindicator shall go before you,
the glory of the Lord shall be your rear guard.
Then you shall call, and the Lord will answer;
you shall cry for help, and he will say, Here I am.
If you remove the yoke from among you,
the pointing of the finger, the speaking of evil,
if you offer your food to the hungry
and satisfy the needs of the afflicted,
then your light shall rise in the darkness
and your gloom be like the noonday.
The word of the Lord. **Thanks be to God.**

Psalm 112

R. **Light rises in the darkness for the upright.**
or **Alleluia!**

Light rises in the darkness for the upright:
gracious, merciful and righteous.
It is well with the person who deals generously and lends,
who conducts their affairs with justice. R.

For the righteous person will never be moved;
they will be remembered forever.
Unafraid of evil tidings;
their heart is firm, secure in the Lord. R.

That person's heart is steady and will not be afraid.
One who has distributed freely, who has given to the poor,
their righteousness endures forever:
their name is exalted in honour. R.

When I came to you, brothers and sisters, I did not come proclaiming the mystery of God to you in lofty words or wisdom. For I decided to know nothing among you except Jesus Christ, and him crucified.

And I came to you in weakness and in fear and in much trembling. My speech and my proclamation were not with plausible words of wisdom, but with a demonstration of the Spirit and of power, so that your faith might rest not on human wisdom but on the power of God.

The word of the Lord. **Thanks be to God.**

Jesus said to his disciples: "You are the salt of the earth; but if salt has lost its taste, how can its saltiness be restored? It is no longer good for anything, but is thrown out and trampled under foot.

"You are the light of the world. A city built on a hill cannot be hidden. No one after lighting a lamp puts it under the bushel basket, but on the lampstand, and it gives light to all in the house. In the same way, let your light shine before human beings, so that they may see your good works and give glory to your Father in heaven."

The Gospel of the Lord. **Praise to you, Lord Jesus Christ.**

When we fast, we eat less than usual. It is a way of sympathizing with the poor, since the poor often don't have enough to eat. In Isaiah, God tells us that when we fast, we must also work to ease the burdens of the poor; otherwise, our fasting is without purpose.

A yoke is a heavy wooden frame that fits over a person's shoulders so they can carry buckets of water or pull a plough. Imagine how good it feels, after a long day working in the hot sun, to remove the yoke! God wants us to help one another remove any burdens we might be carrying.

A vindicator is a person who proves that something is true or right. When we obey God and defend justice, God is our vindicator: God shows that our work is good and right.

Paul tells the people of Corinth that our lives are not based on plausible or believable words of wisdom, but rather on the work of the Spirit. We do not rely on our own power but on the power of God.

Salt brings out the flavours of the foods we eat. In ancient times, salt was an essential preservative for meat, fish and vegetables, since refrigerators did not exist. Because of its long-lasting, preserving nature, salt became a symbol of enduring friendships and a sign of a contract between persons or groups. As "salt of the earth," Jesus' followers bring out the best flavours in life, preserve the Good News of Jesus' loving presence, and are faithful friends of God.

6th Sunday in Ordinary Time

If you choose, you can keep the commandments, and they will save you. If you trust in God, you too shall live, and to act faithfully is a matter of your own choice.

The Lord has placed before you fire and water; stretch out your hand for whichever you choose. Before each person are life and death, good and evil and whichever one chooses, that shall be given.

For great is the wisdom of the Lord; he is mighty in power and sees everything; his eyes are on those who fear him, and he knows every human action. He has not commanded anyone to be wicked, and he has not given anyone permission to sin.

The word of the Lord. **Thanks be to God.**

Psalm 119

℟. **Blessed are those who walk in the law of the Lord!**

Blessed are those whose way is blameless,
who walk in the law of the Lord.
Blessed are those who keep his decrees,
who seek him with their whole heart. ℟.

You have commanded your precepts
to be kept diligently.
O that my ways may be steadfast
in keeping your statutes! ℟.

Deal bountifully with your servant,
so that I may live and observe your word.
Open my eyes, so that I may behold
wondrous things out of your law. ℟.

Teach me, O Lord, the way of your statutes,
and I will observe it to the end.
Give me understanding, that I may keep your law
and observe it with my whole heart. ℟.

Brothers and sisters: Among the mature we do speak wisdom, though it is not a wisdom of this age or of the rulers of this age, who are doomed to perish. But we speak God's wisdom, secret and hidden, which God decreed before the ages for our glory. None of the rulers of this age understood this; for if they had, they would not have crucified the Lord of glory.

As it is written, "What no eye has seen, nor ear heard, nor the human heart conceived, what God has prepared for those who love him." These things God has revealed to us through the Spirit; for the Spirit searches everything, even the depths of God.

The word of the Lord. **Thanks be to God.**

For the shorter version, omit the indented parts.

Jesus said to his disciples: "Do not think that I have come to abolish the Law or the Prophets; I have come not to abolish but to fulfill.

"For truly I tell you, until heaven and earth pass away, not one letter, not one stroke of a letter, will pass from the Law until all is accomplished. Therefore, whoever breaks one of the least of these commandments, and teaches others to do the same, will be called least in the kingdom of heaven; but whoever does them and teaches them will be called great in the kingdom of heaven.

"For I tell you, unless your righteousness exceeds that of the scribes and Pharisees, you will never enter the kingdom of heaven.

"You have heard that it was said to those of ancient times, 'You shall not murder'; and 'whoever murders shall be liable to judgment.' But I say to you that the one who is angry with their brother or sister, will be liable to judgment; and whoever insults their brother or sister, will be liable to the council; and whoever says, 'You fool,' will be liable to the hell of fire.

"So when you are offering your gift at the altar, if you remember that your brother or sister has something against you, leave your gift there before the altar and go; first be reconciled to your brother or sister, and then come and offer your gift.

> "Come to terms quickly with your accuser while the two of you are on the way to court, or your accuser may hand you over to the judge, and the judge to the guard, and you will be thrown into prison. Truly I tell you, you will never get out until you have paid the last penny.

"You have heard that it was said, 'You shall not commit adultery.' But I say to you that everyone who looks at a woman with lust has already committed adultery with her in his heart.

> "If your right eye causes you to sin, tear it out and throw it away; it is better for you to lose one of your members than for your whole body to be thrown into hell. And if your right hand causes you to sin, cut it off and throw it away; it is better for you to lose one of your members than for your whole body to go into hell.

> "It was also said, 'Whoever divorces his wife, let him give her a certificate of divorce.' But I say to you that anyone who divorces his wife, except on the ground of unchastity, causes her to commit adultery; and whoever marries a divorced woman commits adultery.

"Again, you have heard that it was said to those of ancient times, 'You shall not swear falsely, but carry out the vows you have made to the Lord.' But I say to you: Do not swear at all.

> either by heaven, for it is the throne of God, or by the earth, for it is his footstool, or by Jerusalem, for it is the city of the great King. And do not swear by your head, for you cannot make one hair white or black.

"Let your word be 'Yes,' if 'Yes,' or 'No,' if 'No'; anything more than this comes from the evil one."

The Gospel of the Lord. **Praise to you, Lord Jesus Christ.**

The book of Sirach in the Bible was written 200 years before Jesus was born. It tells us that wisdom is respecting God and obeying God's plans for us.

In the Psalm, the writer uses legal terms when he speaks about following God: law, decrees, precepts, statutes. We might think it is hard to follow all these rules, but the Psalmist sees these laws as blessings and life-giving. Jesus says in the Gospel that he has come not to abolish the law but to fulfill it.

To swear is to make a promise relying on something or someone else, and to swear falsely is to break a promise, or to lie when we are making that promise. Because we are not perfect as God is, Jesus says that it is better if we do not make any promises that we cannot keep.

7th Sunday in Ordinary Time

A reading from the book of Leviticus (19.1-2, 17-18)

The Lord spoke to Moses:
"Speak to all the congregation of the children of Israel
and say to them:
'You shall be holy, for I the Lord your God am holy.

"'You shall not hate in your heart anyone of your kin;
you shall reprove your neighbour,
or you will incur guilt yourself.
You shall not take vengeance
or bear a grudge against any of your people,
but you shall love your neighbour as yourself:
I am the Lord.'"

The word of the Lord. **Thanks be to God.**

Psalm 103

R. **The Lord is merciful and gracious.**

Bless the Lord, O my soul,
and all that is within me, bless his holy name.
Bless the Lord, O my soul,
and do not forget all his benefits. R.

It is the Lord who forgives all your iniquity,
who heals all your diseases,
who redeems your life from the Pit,
who crowns you with steadfast love and mercy. R.

The Lord is merciful and gracious,
slow to anger and abounding in steadfast love.
He does not deal with us according to our sins,
nor repay us according to our iniquities. R.

As far as the east is from the west,
so far he removes our transgressions from us.
As a father has compassion for his children,
so the Lord has compassion for those who fear him. R.

A reading from the first Letter of Saint Paul to the Corinthians (3.16-23)

Brothers and sisters: Do you not know that you are God's temple and that God's Spirit dwells in you? If anyone destroys God's temple, God will destroy that person. For God's temple is holy, and you are that temple.

Do not deceive yourselves. If you think that you are wise in this age, you should become fools so that you may become wise. For the wisdom of this world is foolishness with God. For it is written, "He catches the wise in their craftiness," and again, "The Lord knows the thoughts of the wise, that they are futile."

So let no one boast about human beings. For all things are yours—whether Paul or Apollos or Cephas, or the world or life or death, or the present or the future—all belong to you, and you belong to Christ, and Christ belongs to God.

The word of the Lord. **Thanks be to God.**

A reading from the holy Gospel according to Matthew (5.38-48)

Jesus said to his disciples, "You have heard that it was said, 'An eye for an eye and a tooth for a tooth.' But I say to you, Do not resist an evildoer. But if anyone strikes you on the right cheek, turn the other also; and if anyone wants to sue you and take your coat, give your cloak as well; and if anyone forces you to go one mile, go with them also the second mile. Give to everyone who begs from you, and do not refuse anyone who wants to borrow from you.

"You have heard that it was said, 'You shall love your neighbour and hate your enemy.' But I say to you, Love your enemies and pray for those who persecute you, so that you may be children of your Father in heaven; for he makes his sun rise on the evil and on the good, and sends rain on the righteous and on the unrighteous.

"For if you love those who love you, what reward do you have? Do not even the tax collectors do the same? And if you greet only your brothers and sisters, what more are you doing than others? Do not even the Gentiles do the same? Be perfect, therefore, as your heavenly Father is perfect."

The Gospel of the Lord. **Praise to you, Lord Jesus Christ.**

To reprove is to correct someone or show them where they have done something wrong. The Lord tells Moses that we have a duty to do this, but we must do it in a loving way—loving our neighbour as ourselves.

A temple is a place where God dwells—a synagogue or a church, for example. It is startling when Paul reminds us that our bodies and souls are God's temple! We must take good care of our bodies as well as live lives of justice and mercy.

It seems harsh to us when Jesus mentions the saying, "An eye for an eye." But this saying was seen as just and fair, for it meant that compensation for an injury was limited to the value of what had been harmed or taken. What Jesus proposes is radical and surprising, going beyond what is ordinarily seen as acceptable.

In the time of Jesus, most people owned two garments —a coat for daytime use, and a cloak to provide warmth night and day. When Jesus says to offer not only your coat but your cloak as well, he is saying to let go of everything you have!

8th Sunday in Ordinary Time

Zion said, "The Lord has forsaken me,
my Lord has forgotten me."
Can a woman forget her nursing child,
or show no compassion for the child of her womb?
Even these may forget,
yet I will not forget you.

The word of the Lord. **Thanks be to God.**

Psalm 62

R̶ **For God alone my soul waits in silence.**

For God alone my soul waits in silence;
from him comes my salvation.
He alone is my rock and my salvation, my fortress;
I shall never be shaken. R̶

For God alone my soul waits in silence,
for my hope is from him.
He alone is my rock and my salvation, my fortress;
I shall not be shaken. R̶

On God rests my deliverance and my honour;
my mighty rock, my refuge is in God.
Trust in him at all times, O people;
pour out your heart before him. R̶

101

Brothers and sisters: Think of us in this way, as servants of Christ and stewards of God's mysteries. Moreover, it is required of stewards that they be found trustworthy.

But with me it is a very small thing that I should be judged by you or by any human court. I do not even judge myself. I am not aware of anything against myself, but I am not thereby acquitted. It is the Lord who judges me.

Therefore do not pronounce judgment before the time, before the Lord comes, who will bring to light the things now hidden in darkness and will disclose the purposes of the heart. Then each one will receive commendation from God.

The word of the Lord. **Thanks be to God.**

Jesus taught his disciples, saying. "No one can serve two masters; for a slave will either hate the one and love the other, or be devoted to the one and despise the other. You cannot serve God and wealth.

"Therefore I tell you, do not worry about your life, what you will eat or what you will drink, or about your body, what you will wear. Is not life more than food, and the body more than clothing?

"Look at the birds of the air; they neither sow nor reap nor gather into barns, and yet your heavenly Father feeds them. Are you not of more value than they? And can any one of you by worrying add a single hour to their span of life?

"And why do you worry about clothing? Consider the lilies of the field, how they grow; they neither toil nor spin, yet I tell you, even Solomon in all his glory was not clothed like one of these. But if God so clothes the grass of the field, which is alive today and tomorrow is thrown into the oven, will he not much more clothe you—you of little faith?

"Therefore do not worry, saying, 'What will we eat?' or 'What will we drink?' or 'What will we wear?' For it is the Gentiles who strive for all these things; and indeed your heavenly Father knows that you need all these things. But strive first for the kingdom of God and his righteousness, and all these things will be given to you as well.

"So do not worry about tomorrow, for tomorrow will bring worries of its own. Today's trouble is enough for today."

The Gospel of the Lord. **Praise to you, Lord Jesus Christ.**

Zion was the name of a hill in Jerusalem, where the temple was built, but the city itself was often called Zion. Zion is another way of naming the entire nation, the whole people of God.

Stewards are people who are given the responsibility to care for and manage things that belong to someone else. They are given this task because they are honest and trustworthy. Paul tells us that as Christians we are stewards of God's mysteries.

Solomon became king of Israel after his father David. Solomon is famous for his wisdom and for the beauty and magnificence of his royal court.

The land around Israel is naturally dry and brown most of the year. When wild grasses and flowers bloom, they live a short time and then wither—they are alive today and gone shortly after. Jesus uses the example of these plants to show us how insignificant are the things we worry so much about.

9th Sunday in Ordinary Time

Moses said to the people: "You shall put these words of mine in your heart and soul, and you shall bind them as a sign on your hand, and fix them as an emblem on your forehead.

"See, I am setting before you today a blessing and a curse: the blessing, if you obey the commandments of the Lord your God that I am commanding you today; and the curse, if you do not obey the commandments of the Lord your God, but turn from the way that I am commanding you today, to follow other gods that you have not known.

"You must diligently observe all the statutes and ordinances that I am setting before you today."

The word of the Lord. **Thanks be to God.**

Psalm 31

R. **Lord, be a rock of refuge for me.**

In you, O Lord, I seek refuge;
do not let me ever be put to shame;
in your righteousness deliver me.
Incline your ear to me; rescue me speedily. R.

Be a rock of refuge for me,
a strong fortress to save me.
You are indeed my rock and my fortress;
for your name's sake lead me and guide me. R.

Let your face shine upon your servant;
save me in your steadfast love.
Be strong, and let your heart take courage,
all you who wait for the Lord. R.

Brothers and sisters: Now, apart from Law, the righteousness of God has been disclosed, and is attested by the Law and the Prophets, the righteousness of God through faith in Jesus Christ for all who believe.

For there is no distinction, since all have sinned and fall short of the glory of God; they are now justified by his grace as a gift, through the redemption that is in Christ Jesus, whom God put forward as a sacrifice of atonement by his blood.

For we hold that a person is justified by faith apart from works prescribed by the Law.

The word of the Lord. **Thanks be to God.**

Jesus went up the mountain with his disciples. He sat down and began to teach them: "Not everyone who says to me, 'Lord, Lord,' will enter the kingdom of heaven, but only the one who does the will of my Father in heaven. On that day many will say to me, 'Lord, Lord, did we not prophesy in your name, and cast out demons in your name, and do many deeds of power in your name?' Then I will declare to them, 'I never knew you; go away from me, you evildoers.'

"Everyone then who hears these words of mine and acts on them will be like a wise man who built his house on rock. The rain fell, the floods came, and the winds blew and beat on that house, but it did not fall, because it had been founded on rock. And everyone who hears these words of mine and does not act on them will be like a foolish man who built his house on sand. The rain fell, and the floods came, and the winds blew and beat against that house, and it fell—and great was its fall!"

The Gospel of the Lord. **Praise to you, Lord Jesus Christ.**

Deuteronomy is a Greek word meaning 'the second law.' This book in the Bible tells us that God is one and so the People of God must be united.

When the Israelites were having a hard time but their neighbours were enjoying good times, God's people were tempted to adore the neighbouring gods instead. They hoped that if they worshipped other gods, things would get better. Even though God's People turned their backs on him, God remained faithful to them.

The statutes and ordinances are the commandments that God gave to Moses. They show God's people how to live in peace with each other and be faithful to God.

Paul says we are justified or brought back to friendship with God by his grace. God, through Jesus, forgives us and welcomes us in baptism.

In the kingdom of heaven, all people will be brought together in Jesus. We will all live like brothers and sisters, sharing in God's love.

A faithful follower of Jesus listens to his words and then acts on them. We must put our faith into practice, especially in helping the poor and respecting others.

Ash Wednesday Service

The ceremony may consist of a brief scripture service as outlined here.

Gathering Prayers

The Word

1st Reading: *Joel 2.12-18*

Psalm 51: R. **Have mercy, O Lord, for we have sinned.**

2nd Reading: *2 Corinthians 5.20 – 6.2*

Gospel: *Matthew 6.1-6, 16-18*

Blessing and Giving of Ashes

Dear friends in Christ, let us ask our Father to bless these ashes which we will use as the mark of our repentance. *(Pause)* Lord, bless the sinner who asks for your forgiveness and bless all those who receive these ashes. May they keep this Lenten season in preparation for the joy of Easter.

While everyone comes forward to receive ashes, an appropriate song may be sung. The priest says to each person:

1   Turn away from sin and be faithful to the gospel.

or

2   Remember that you are dust and to dust you will return.

Lord's Prayer (page 24 or 315)

Closing Hymn

1st Sunday of Lent

The Lord God formed man from the dust of the ground, and breathed into his nostrils the breath of life; and the man became a living being. And the Lord God planted a garden in Eden, in the east; and there he put the man whom he had formed. Out of the ground the Lord God made to grow every tree that is pleasant to the sight and good for food, the tree of life also in the midst of the garden, and the tree of the knowledge of good and evil.

And the Lord God commanded the man, "You may freely eat of every tree of the garden; but of the tree of the knowledge of good and evil you shall not eat, for in the day that you eat of it you shall die."

Then the Lord God said, "It is not good that the man should be alone; I will make him a helper as his partner." And the man and his wife were both naked, and were not ashamed.

Now the serpent was more crafty than any other wild animal that the Lord God had made. He said to the woman, "Did God say, 'You shall not eat from any tree in the garden'?" The woman said to the serpent, "We may eat of the fruit of the trees in the garden; but God said, 'You shall not eat of the fruit of the tree that is in the middle of the garden, nor shall you touch it, or you shall die.'" But the serpent said to the woman, "You will not die; for God knows that when you eat of it your eyes will be opened, and you will be like God, knowing good and evil." So when the woman saw that the tree was good for food, and that it was a delight to the eyes, and that the tree was to be desired to make one wise, she took of its fruit and ate; and she also gave some to her husband, who was with her, and he ate.

Then the eyes of both were opened, and they knew that they were naked; and they sewed fig leaves together and made loincloths for themselves.

The word of the Lord. **Thanks be to God.**

R̦ **Have mercy, O Lord, for we have sinned.**

Have mercy on me, O God,
according to your steadfast love;
according to your abundant mercy
blot out my transgressions.
Wash me thoroughly from my iniquity,
and cleanse me from my sin. R̦

For I know my transgressions,
and my sin is ever before me.
Against you, you alone, have I sinned,
and done what is evil in your sight. R̦

Create in me a clean heart, O God,
and put a new and right spirit within me.
Do not cast me away from your presence,
and do not take your holy spirit from me. R̦

Restore to me the joy of your salvation,
and sustain in me a willing spirit.
O Lord, open my lips,
and my mouth will declare your praise. R̦

A reading from the Letter of Saint Paul to the Romans (5.12-19)

For the shorter version, omit the indented parts.

Brothers and sisters: Just as sin came into the world through one man, and death came through sin, so death spread to all people, because all have sinned.

Sin was indeed in the world before the law, but sin is not reckoned when there is no law. Yet death exercised dominion from Adam to Moses, even over those whose sins were not like the transgression of Adam, who is a type of the one who was to come.

But the free gift is not like the trespass. For if the many died through the one man's trespass, much more surely have the grace of God and the free gift in the grace of the one man,

Jesus Christ, abounded for the many. And the free gift is not like the effect of the one man's sin. For the judgment following one trespass brought condemnation, but the free gift following many trespasses brings justification.

If, because of the one man's trespass, death exercised dominion through that one, much more surely will those who receive the abundance of grace and the free gift of righteousness exercise dominion in life through the one man, Jesus Christ.

Therefore just as one man's trespass led to condemnation for all people, so one man's act of righteousness leads to justification and life for all people. For just as by the one man's disobedience the many were made sinners, so by the one man's obedience the many will be made righteous.

The word of the Lord. **Thanks be to God.**

A reading from the holy Gospel according to Matthew
(4.1-11)

Jesus was led up by the Spirit into the wilderness to be tempted by the devil. He fasted forty days and forty nights, and afterwards he was famished. The tempter came and said to him, "If you are the Son of God, command these stones to become loaves of bread." But he answered, "It is written, 'Man does not live by bread alone, but by every word that comes from the mouth of God.'"

Then the devil took him to the holy city and placed him on the pinnacle of the temple, saying to him, "If you are the Son of God, throw yourself down; for it is written, 'He will command his Angels concerning you,' and 'On their hands they will bear you up, so that you will not dash your foot against a stone.'" Jesus said to him, "Again it is written, 'Do not put the Lord your God to the test.'"

Again, the devil took him to a very high mountain and showed him all the kingdoms of the world and their splendour; and he said to him, "All these I will give you, if you will fall down and worship me." Jesus said to him, "Away with you, Satan! for it is written, 'Worship the Lord your God, and serve only him.'"

Then the devil left him, and suddenly Angels came and waited on him.

The Gospel of the Lord. **Praise to you, Lord Jesus Christ.**

Genesis is the first book of the Bible. It tells many stories, including the stories of creation, Adam and Eve, the flood, Abraham, and the people's faith in God. These stories help us understand that God loves us and wants us to love him too.

God breathed life into the first human being. This is a way of showing us how we share God's life.

It is hard to understand good and evil. In this story, we see evil as an enemy of God's, an enemy who tempts us to turn away from our Creator.

In this part of Genesis, the enemy of God takes the shape of a serpent.

The letter of Saint Paul to the Romans was written to the small community of Christians who lived in Rome. Paul wanted to visit them, so he sent them this letter ahead, to encourage them and to remind them of the teachings of Jesus.

When we are tempted, we may do something we know is wrong.

The pinnacle of the temple was its highest point.

When we worship God, we praise him for his love.

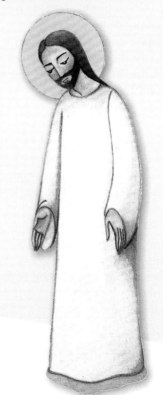

2nd Sunday of Lent

GENINA

A reading from the book of Genesis (12.1-4)

The Lord said to Abram, "Go from your country and your kindred and your father's house to the land that I will show you. I will make of you a great nation, and I will bless you, and make your name great, so that you will be a blessing. I will bless those who bless you, and the one who curses you I will curse; and in you all the families of the earth shall be blessed."

So Abram went, as the Lord had told him.

The word of the Lord. **Thanks be to God.**

Psalm 33

R. **Let your love be upon us, Lord, even as we hope in you.**

The word of the Lord is upright,
and all his work is done in faithfulness.
He loves righteousness and justice;
the earth is full of the steadfast love of the Lord. R.

Truly the eye of the Lord is on those who fear him,
on those who hope in his steadfast love,
to deliver their soul from death,
and to keep them alive in famine. R.

Our soul waits for the Lord;
he is our help and shield.
Let your steadfast love, O Lord, be upon us,
even as we hope in you. R.

A reading from the second Letter of Saint Paul to Timothy (1.8-10)

Brothers and sisters: Join with me in suffering for the Gospel, relying on the power of God, who saved us and called us with a holy calling, not according to our works but according to his own purpose and grace.

This grace was given to us in Christ Jesus before the ages began, but it has now been revealed through the appearing of our Saviour Christ Jesus, who abolished death and brought life and immortality to light through the Gospel.

The word of the Lord. **Thanks be to God.**

A reading from the holy Gospel according to Matthew (17.1-9)

Jesus took with him Peter and James and his brother John and led them up a high mountain, by themselves. And he was transfigured before them, and his face shone like the sun, and his clothes became dazzling white. Suddenly there appeared to them Moses and Elijah, talking with him.

Then Peter said to Jesus, "Lord, it is good for us to be here; if you wish, I will make three dwellings here, one for you, one for Moses, and one for Elijah."

While he was still speaking, suddenly a bright cloud overshadowed them, and from the cloud a voice said, "This is my Son, the Beloved; with him I am well pleased; listen to him!"

When the disciples heard this, they fell to the ground and were overcome by fear. But Jesus came and touched them, saying, "Get up and do not be afraid." And when they looked up, they saw no one except Jesus himself alone.

As they were coming down the mountain, Jesus ordered them, "Tell no one about the vision until after the Son of Man has been raised from the dead."

The Gospel of the Lord. **Praise to you, Lord Jesus Christ.**

Abram had true faith in God. God promised him that he would become the head of a huge family. God then gave him a new name: Abraham.

Abraham's descendants (including us) became a great nation, as God had promised. The people of God all over the world are also a great nation, brothers and sisters in Christ.

Timothy was a friend of Paul's. He helped Paul to spread the gospel and was in charge of the church in Ephesus. In the New Testament there are two letters to Timothy.

When we live the life Jesus has planned for us, we are responding to his calling. Little by little, God opens our ears to hear this call and follow Jesus.

Because Jesus died and rose again, and because we are united with Jesus, we share in his immortality (life without death).

When Jesus was transfigured, he looked different somehow. His friends see who Jesus really is: the Son of God.

The prophet Elijah lived about 900 years before Jesus. He taught the people about God.

3rd Sunday of Lent

In the wilderness the people thirsted for water; and the people complained against Moses and said, "Why did you bring us out of Egypt, to kill us and our children and livestock with thirst?" So Moses cried out to the Lord, "What shall I do with this people? They are almost ready to stone me."

The Lord said to Moses, "Go on ahead of the people, and take some of the elders of Israel with you; take in your hand the staff with which you struck the Nile, and go. I will be standing there in front of you on the rock at Horeb. Strike the rock, and water will come out of it, so that the people may drink." Moses did so, in the sight of the elders of Israel.

He called the place Massah and Meribah, because the children of Israel quarrelled and tested the Lord, saying, "Is the Lord among us or not?"

The word of the Lord. **Thanks be to God.**

Psalm 95

℟. **O that today you would listen to the voice of the Lord. Do not harden your hearts!**

O come, let us sing to the Lord;
let us make a joyful noise to the rock of our salvation!
Let us come into his presence with thanksgiving;
let us make a joyful noise to him with songs of praise! ℟.

O come, let us worship and bow down,
let us kneel before the Lord, our Maker!
For he is our God, and we are the people of his pasture,
and the sheep of his hand. ℟.

O that today you would listen to his voice!
Do not harden your hearts, as at Meribah,
as on the day at Massah in the wilderness,
when your ancestors tested me,
and put me to the proof,
though they had seen my work. ℟.

A reading from the Letter of Saint Paul to the Romans (5.1-2, 5-8)

Brothers and sisters: Since we are justified by faith, we have peace with God through our Lord Jesus Christ, through whom we have obtained access to this grace in which we stand; and we boast in our hope of sharing the glory of God.

And hope does not disappoint us, because God's love has been poured into our hearts through the Holy Spirit that has been given to us. For while we were still weak, at the right time Christ died for the ungodly. Indeed, rarely will anyone die for a righteous person—though perhaps for a good person someone might actually dare to die. But God proves his love for us in that while we still were sinners Christ died for us.

The word of the Lord. **Thanks be to God.**

A reading from the holy Gospel according to John (4.5-42)

For the shorter reading, omit the indented parts.

Jesus came to a Samaritan city called Sychar, near the plot of ground that Jacob had given to his son Joseph. Jacob's well was there, and Jesus, tired out by his journey, was sitting by the well. It was about noon.

A Samaritan woman came to draw water, and Jesus said to her, "Give me a drink." (His disciples had gone to the city to buy food.)

The Samaritan woman said to him, "How is it that you, a Jew, ask a drink of me, a woman of Samaria?" (Jews do not share things in common with Samaritans.) Jesus answered her, "If you knew the gift of God, and who it is that is saying to you, 'Give me a drink,' you would have asked him, and he would have given you living water."

The woman said to him, "Sir, you have no bucket, and the well is deep. Where do you get that living water? Are you greater than our father Jacob, who gave us the well, and with his children and his flocks drank from it?" Jesus said to her,

"Everyone who drinks of this water will be thirsty again, but the one who drinks of the water that I will give will never be thirsty. The water that I will give him will become in him a spring of water gushing up to eternal life." The woman said to him, "Sir, give me this water, so that I may never be thirsty or have to keep coming here to draw water."

Jesus said to her, "Go, call your husband, and come back." The woman answered him, "I have no husband." Jesus said to her, "You are right in saying, 'I have no husband'; for you have had five husbands, and the one you have now is not your husband. What you have said is true!" The woman said to him, "Sir,

"I see that you are a Prophet. Our ancestors worshipped on this mountain, but you say that the place where people must worship is in Jerusalem."

Jesus said to her, "Woman, believe me, the hour is coming when you will worship the Father neither on this mountain nor in Jerusalem. You worship what you do not know; we worship what we know, for salvation is from the Jews. But the hour is coming, and is now here, when the true worshippers will worship the Father in spirit and truth, for the Father seeks such as these to worship him. God is spirit, and those who worship him must worship in spirit and truth."

The woman said to him, "I know that the Messiah is coming" (who is called the Christ). "When he comes, he will proclaim all things to us." Jesus said to her, "I am he, the one who is speaking to you."

Just then his disciples came. They were astonished that he was speaking with a woman, but no one said, "What do you want?" or, "Why are you speaking with her?" Then the woman left her water jar and went back to the city. She said to the people, "Come and see a man who told me everything I have ever done! He cannot be the Messiah, can he?" They left the city and were on their way to him. Meanwhile the disciples were urging him, "Rabbi, eat something." But he said to them, "I have food to eat that you do not know about." So the disciples said to one another, "Surely no one has brought him something to eat?"

Jesus said to them, "My food is to do the will of him who sent me and to complete his work. Do you not say, 'Four months more, then comes the harvest'? But I tell you, look around you, and see how the fields are ripe for harvesting. The reaper is already receiving wages and is gathering fruit for eternal life, so that sower and reaper may rejoice together. For here the saying holds true, 'One sows and another reaps.' I sent you to reap that for which you did not labour. Others have laboured, and you have entered into their labour."

Many Samaritans from that city believed in Jesus because of the woman's testimony, "He told me everything I have ever done." So when the Samaritans came to him, they asked him to stay with them; and he stayed there two days. And many more believed because of his word. They said to the woman, "It is no longer because of what you said that we believe, for we have heard for ourselves, and we know that this is truly the Saviour of the world."

The Gospel of the Lord. **Praise to you, Lord Jesus Christ.**

The book of Exodus is the second book of the Bible. It tells the story of how God freed his people from slavery in Egypt. God made a promise or covenant with them and gave them the Ten Commandments to show them how to live well.

A staff is large stick or cane used by a shepherd and other herdsmen. It can also be used as a walking stick. It is a symbol of authority carried by a leader.

When we hurt others, we break our friendship with God. Jesus came to restore our friendship with God, and we are justified or brought back to God by our faith in Jesus.

We have hope or confidence that God will fulfill his promises. Hope is one of the three great Christian virtues. The other two are faith and love.

The holy Gospel according to John tells us about the life, death and resurrection of Jesus. It was written about 60 years after Jesus died. John's Gospel includes some stories and sayings of Jesus that are not in the other three gospels (Matthew, Mark and Luke).

Jacob, also called Israel, was the son of Isaac, who was the son of Abraham. The twelve tribes of Israel are all descended from Jacob.

When Jesus says to worship the Father in spirit and truth, he is reminding us that God does not want us to kill living things when we worship. God would rather we bring him our hearts full of love.

Jesus and his disciples spoke Aramaic. Messiah is an Aramaic word meaning 'anointed.' The chosen person was anointed or blessed with holy oil and given a special mission. The Greek word for 'anointed' is 'Christ.'

4th Sunday of Lent

GENINA

The Lord said to Samuel, "Fill your horn with oil and set out; I will send you to Jesse of Bethlehem, for I have provided for myself a king among his sons."

When the sons of Jesse came, Samuel looked on Eliab and thought, "Surely the Lord's anointed is now before the Lord." But the Lord said to Samuel, "Do not look on his appearance or on the height of his stature, because I have rejected him; for the Lord does not see as the human sees; the human looks on the outward appearance, but the Lord looks on the heart."

Jesse made seven of his sons pass before Samuel, and Samuel said to Jesse, "The Lord has not chosen any of these." Samuel said to Jesse, "Are all your sons here?" And he said, "There remains yet the youngest, but he is keeping the sheep." And Samuel said to Jesse, "Send and bring him; for we will not sit down until he comes here." Jesse sent and brought David in. Now he was ruddy, and had beautiful eyes, and was handsome. The Lord said, "Rise and anoint him; for this is the one."

Then Samuel took the horn of oil, and anointed him in the presence of his brothers; and the spirit of the Lord came mightily upon David from that day forward.

The word of the Lord. **Thanks be to God.**

Psalm 23

℟. **The Lord is my shepherd; I shall not want.**

The Lord is my shepherd, I shall not want.
He makes me lie down in green pastures;
he leads me beside still waters;
he restores my soul. ℟.

He leads me in right paths for his name's sake.
Even though I walk through the darkest valley,
 I fear no evil;
for you are with me;
your rod and your staff—they comfort me. ℟.

You prepare a table before me
in the presence of my enemies;
you anoint my head with oil;
my cup overflows. R̸

Surely goodness and mercy shall follow me
all the days of my life,
and I shall dwell in the house of the Lord
my whole life long. R̸

A reading from the Letter of Saint Paul to the Ephesians (5.8-14)

Brothers and sisters: Once you were darkness, but now in the Lord you are light. Live as children of light—for the fruit of the light is found in all that is good and right and true.

Try to find out what is pleasing to the Lord. Take no part in the unfruitful works of darkness, but instead expose them. For it is shameful even to mention what such people do secretly; but everything exposed by the light becomes visible, for everything that becomes visible is light. Therefore it is said, "Sleeper, awake! Rise from the dead, and Christ will shine on you."

The word of the Lord. **Thanks be to God.**

A reading from the holy Gospel according to John (9.1-41)

For the shorter version, omit the indented parts.

As Jesus walked along, he saw a man blind from birth.

His disciples asked him, "Rabbi, who sinned, this man or his parents, that he was born blind?"

Jesus answered, "Neither this man nor his parents sinned; he was born blind so that God's works might be revealed in him. We must work the works of him who sent me while it is day; night is coming when no one can work. As long as I am in the world, I am the light of the world." When he had said this,

He spat on the ground and made mud with the saliva and spread the mud on the man's eyes, saying to him, "Go, wash in the pool of Siloam" (which means Sent).

Then the man who was blind went and washed, and came back able to see. The neighbours and those who had seen him before as a beggar began to ask, "Is this not the man who used to sit and beg?" Some were saying, "It is he." Others were saying, "No, but it is someone like him." He kept saying, "I am the man."

> But they kept asking him, "Then how were your eyes opened?" He answered, "The man called Jesus made mud, spread it on my eyes, and said to me, 'Go to Siloam and wash.' Then I went and washed and received my sight." They said to him, "Where is he?" He said, "I do not know."

They brought to the Pharisees the man who had formerly been blind. Now it was a Sabbath day when Jesus made the mud and opened his eyes. Then the Pharisees also began to ask him how he had received his sight. He said to them, "He put mud on my eyes. Then I washed, and now I see." Some of the Pharisees said, "This man is not from God, for he does not observe the Sabbath." But others said, "How can a man who is a sinner perform such signs?" And they were divided. So they said again to the blind man, "What do you say about him? It was your eyes he opened." He said, "He is a Prophet."

> They did not believe that he had been blind and had received his sight until they called the parents of the man who had received his sight and asked them, "Is this your son, who you say was born blind? How then does he now see?" His parents answered, "We know that this is our son, and that he was born blind; but we do not know how it is that now he sees, nor do we know who opened his eyes. Ask him; he is of age. He will speak for himself." His parents said this because they were afraid of the Jewish authorities, who had already agreed that anyone who confessed Jesus to be the Messiah would be put out of the synagogue. Therefore his parents said, "He is of age; ask him."

> So for the second time they called the man who had been blind, and they said to him, "Give glory to God! We know that this man is a sinner." He answered, "I do not know whether he is a sinner. One thing I do know, that though I was blind, now I see." They said to him, "What did he do to you? How did he open your eyes?" He answered them, "I have told you already, and you would not listen. Why do you want to hear it again? Do you also want to become his disciples?"

Then they reviled him, saying, "You are his disciple, but we are disciples of Moses. We know that God has spoken to Moses, but as for this man, we do not know where he comes from."

The man answered, "Here is an astonishing thing! You do not know where he comes from, and yet he opened my eyes. We know that God does not listen to sinners, but he does listen to one who worships him and obeys his will. Never since the world began has it been heard that anyone opened the eyes of a person born blind. If this man were not from God, he could do nothing."

They answered him, "You were born entirely in sins, and are you trying to teach us?" And they drove him out.

Jesus heard that they had driven him out, and when he found him, he said, "Do you believe in the Son of Man?" He answered, "And who is he, sir? Tell me, so that I may believe in him." Jesus said to him, "You have seen him, and the one speaking with you is he." He said, "Lord, I believe." And he worshipped him.

Jesus said, "I came into this world for judgment so that those who do not see may see, and those who do see may become blind." Some of the Pharisees near him heard this and said to him, "Surely we are not blind, are we?" Jesus said to them, "If you were blind, you would have no sin. But now that you say, 'We see,' your sin remains."

The Gospel of the Lord. **Praise to you, Lord Jesus Christ.**

Samuel, a prophet and judge in Israel, was born over 1,000 years before Jesus. The Lord chose Samuel to anoint the first king of Israel, Saul. He also anointed David, who was king after Saul. The Bible contains two books in his name: First Samuel and Second Samuel.

To anoint means to 'bless with oil.' In the Bible it can also mean to give someone a mission, an important job. Christians are anointed at baptism and confirmation: our mission is to love people as God loves them.

The Ephesians were a group of Christians in the city of Ephesus. A letter Paul wrote to them is now part of the Bible. Ephesus is located in modern-day Turkey.

In the time of Jesus, if someone was born blind, people assumed this was because God was punishing the parents for something they had done wrong. Jesus heals the man born blind to show that he has power over evil.

The Pharisees were Jewish leaders who tried to follow the letter of the law, but sometimes forgot to live by love. Jesus pointed out this lack of love.

The Sabbath is the day of the week when human beings rest as God did on the seventh day of creation. It is a chance for us to spend time praising God and enjoying creation. One of the Ten Commandments instructs us to keep the Sabbath holy.

April 10

5th Sunday of Lent

GENINA

A reading from the book of the Prophet Ezekiel

(37.12-14)

Thus says the Lord God: "I am going to open your graves, and bring you up from your graves, O my people; and I will bring you back to the land of Israel. And you shall know that I am the Lord, when I open your graves, and bring you up from your graves, O my people.

"I will put my spirit within you, and you shall live, and I will place you on your own soil; then you shall know that I, the Lord, have spoken and will act," says the Lord.

The word of the Lord. **Thanks be to God.**

Psalm 130

R. **With the Lord there is steadfast love and great power to redeem.**

Out of the depths I cry to you, O Lord.
Lord, hear my voice!
Let your ears be attentive
to the voice of my supplications! R.

If you, O Lord, should mark iniquities,
Lord, who could stand?
But there is forgiveness with you,
so that you may be revered. R.

I wait for the Lord,
my soul waits, and in his word I hope;
my soul waits for the Lord
more than watchmen for the morning. R.

For with the Lord there is steadfast love,
and with him is great power to redeem.
It is he who will redeem Israel
from all its iniquities. R.

Brothers and sisters: Those who are in the flesh cannot please God. But you are not in the flesh; you are in the Spirit, since the Spirit of God dwells in you. Anyone who does not have the Spirit of Christ does not belong to him.

But if Christ is in you, though the body is dead because of sin, the Spirit is life because of righteousness.

If the Spirit of God who raised Jesus from the dead dwells in you, he who raised Christ from the dead will give life to your mortal bodies also through his Spirit that dwells in you.

The word of the Lord. **Thanks be to God.**

For the shorter version, omit the indented parts.

Now a certain man, Lazarus, was ill. He was from Bethany, the village of Mary and her sister Martha. Mary was the one who anointed the Lord with perfume and wiped his feet with her hair; her brother Lazarus was ill. So

The sisters of Lazarus sent a message to Jesus, "Lord, he whom you love is ill." But when Jesus heard this, he said, "This illness does not lead to death; rather it is for God's glory, so that the Son of God may be glorified through it." Accordingly, though Jesus loved Martha and her sister and Lazarus, after having heard that Lazarus was ill, he stayed two days longer in the place where he was. Then after this he said to the disciples, "Let us go to Judea again."

The disciples said to him, "Rabbi, the people there were just now trying to stone you, and are you going there again?" Jesus answered, "Are there not twelve hours of daylight? Those who walk during the day do not stumble, because they see the light of this world. But those who walk at night stumble, because the light is not in them."

After saying this, he told them, "Our friend Lazarus has fallen asleep, but I am going there to awaken him." The disciples said to him, "Lord, if he has fallen asleep, he will be all right." Jesus, however, had been speaking about his death, but they thought that he was referring merely to sleep. Then Jesus told them plainly, "Lazarus is dead. For your sake I am glad I was not there, so that you may believe. But let us go to him." Thomas, who was called the Twin, said to his fellow disciples, "Let us also go, that we may die with him."

When Jesus arrived, he found that Lazarus had already been in the tomb four days.

Now Bethany was near Jerusalem, some two miles away, and many Jews had come to Martha and Mary to console them about their brother.

When Martha heard that Jesus was coming, she went and met him, while Mary stayed at home. Martha said to Jesus, "Lord, if you had been here, my brother would not have died. But even now I know that God will give you whatever you ask of him." Jesus said to her, "Your brother will rise again." Martha said to him, "I know that he will rise again in the resurrection on the last day." Jesus said to her, "I am the resurrection and the life. Whoever believes in me, even though they die, will live, and everyone who lives and believes in me will never die. Do you believe this?" She said to him, "Yes, Lord, I believe that you are the Christ, the Son of God, the one coming into the world."

When she had said this, she went back and called her sister Mary, and told her privately, "The Teacher is here and is calling for you." And when Mary heard it, she got up quickly and went to him. Now Jesus had not yet come to the village, but was still at the place where Martha had met him. The Jews who were with her in the house, consoling her, saw Mary get up quickly and go out. They followed her because they thought that she was going to the tomb to weep there.

When Mary came where Jesus was and saw him, she knelt at his feet and said to him, "Lord, if you had been here, my brother would not have died." When Jesus saw her weeping, and the Jews who came with her also weeping,

Jesus was greatly disturbed in spirit and deeply moved. He said, "Where have you laid him?" They said to him, "Lord, come and see." Jesus began to weep. So the Jews said, "See how he loved him!" But some of them said, "Could not he who opened the eyes of the blind man have kept this man from dying?"

Then Jesus, again greatly disturbed, came to the tomb. It was a cave, and a stone was lying against it. Jesus said, "Take away the stone." Martha, the sister of the dead man, said to him, "Lord, already there is a stench because he has been dead four days." Jesus said to her, "Did I not tell you that if you believed, you would see the glory of God?" So they took away the stone. And Jesus looked upward and said, "Father, I thank you for having heard me. I knew that you always hear me, but I have said this for the sake of the crowd standing here, so that they may believe that you sent me."

When he had said this, he cried with a loud voice, "Lazarus, come out!" The dead man came out, his hands and feet bound with strips of cloth, and his face wrapped in a cloth. Jesus said to them, "Unbind him, and let him go."

Many of the Jews therefore, who had come with Mary and had seen what Jesus did, believed in him.

The Gospel of the Lord. **Praise to you, Lord Jesus Christ.**

Ezekiel was one of the most important prophets in Israel. He lived during a time when many of the people of Jerusalem were taken prisoner and forced to live in another place, Babylon. The king and Ezekiel were taken away, too. Ezekiel helped the people follow God's ways even though they were far from home.

The people of Israel lived in exile in Babylon and were very unhappy. Through the prophet Ezekiel, God promised to bring the people back to Israel. God said, "I am going to open your graves" and bring new life.

In the Bible, God is called the Lord because God is more powerful than all human power.

The Spirit of God, or the Holy Spirit, is the third person of the Holy Trinity. The Spirit of God is always present in our hearts and in the Church, helping us to live like brothers and sisters.

The sisters of Lazarus were Martha and Mary, and all three were Jesus' friends. They lived in Bethany, just a few kilometres from Jerusalem (see the map, page 320). When Jesus had visited them before, he had reminded them that it was more important to listen to the word of God than to worry about daily chores.

When Jesus says that Lazarus will rise again, he is speaking of the resurrection of the dead when Jesus comes again.

Passion Sunday

When they had come near Jerusalem and had reached Bethphage, at the Mount of Olives, Jesus sent two disciples, saying to them, "Go into the village ahead of you, and immediately you will find a donkey tied, and a colt with her; untie them and bring them to me. If anyone says anything to you, just say this, 'The Lord needs them.' And he will send them immediately."

This took place to fulfill what had been spoken through the Prophet, saying, "Tell the daughter of Zion, Look, your king is coming to you, humble, and mounted on a donkey, and on a colt, the foal of a donkey."

The disciples went and did as Jesus had directed them; they brought the donkey and the colt, and put their cloaks on them, and he sat on them. A very large crowd spread their cloaks on the road, and others cut branches from the trees and spread them on the road. The crowds that went ahead of him and that followed were shouting, "Hosanna to the Son of David! Blessed is the one who comes in the name of the Lord! Hosanna in the highest heaven!"

When Jesus entered Jerusalem, the whole city was in turmoil, asking, "Who is this?" The crowds were saying, "This is the Prophet Jesus from Nazareth in Galilee."

The Gospel of the Lord.
**Praise to you,
Lord Jesus Christ.**

The servant of the Lord said:
"The Lord God has given me the tongue of a teacher,
that I may know how to sustain the weary with a word.
Morning by morning he wakens—
wakens my ear to listen as those who are taught.

"The Lord God has opened my ear,
and I was not rebellious,
I did not turn backward.

"I gave my back to those who struck me,
and my cheeks to those who pulled out the beard;
I did not hide my face
from insult and spitting.

"The Lord God helps me;
therefore I have not been disgraced;
therefore I have set my face like flint,
and I know that I shall not be put to shame."

The word of the Lord. **Thanks be to God.**

Psalm 22

R̰. **My God, my God, why have you forsaken me?**

All who see me mock at me;
they make mouths at me, they shake their heads;
"Commit your cause to the Lord; let him deliver;
let him rescue the one in whom he delights!" R̰.

For dogs are all around me;
a company of evildoers encircles me.
My hands and feet have shrivelled;
I can count all my bones. R̰.

They divide my clothes among themselves,
and for my clothing they cast lots.
But you, O Lord, do not be far away!
O my help, come quickly to my aid! R̰.

I will tell of your name to my brothers and sisters;
in the midst of the congregation I will praise you:
You who fear the Lord, praise him!
All you offspring of Jacob, glorify him;
stand in awe of him, all you offspring of Israel! R̰.

139

Christ Jesus, though he was in the form of God, did not regard equality with God as something to be exploited, but emptied himself, taking the form of a slave, being born in human likeness. And being found in human form, he humbled himself and became obedient to the point of death—even death on a cross.

Therefore God highly exalted him and gave him the name that is above every name, so that at the name of Jesus every knee should bend, in heaven and on earth and under the earth, and every tongue should confess that Jesus Christ is Lord, to the glory of God the Father.

The word of the Lord. **Thanks be to God.**

A reading from the holy Gospel according to Matthew (26.14 – 27.66)

Several readers may proclaim the passion narrative today.
N indicates the narrator, J the words of Jesus, and S the words
of other speakers. The shorter version begins (page 145) and ends
(page 148) at the asterisks.

N The Passion of our Lord Jesus Christ according to Matthew.

One of the twelve, who was called Judas Iscariot, went to the chief priests and said,

S *What will you give me if I betray him to you?*

N They paid him thirty pieces of silver. And from that moment he began to look for an opportunity to betray him.

On the first day of Unleavened Bread the disciples came to Jesus, saying,

S *Where do you want us to make the preparations for you to eat the Passover?*

J **Go into the city to a certain man, and say to him, "The Teacher says, My time is near; I will keep the Passover at your house with my disciples."**

N So the disciples did as Jesus had directed them, and they prepared the Passover meal.

When it was evening, he took his place with the twelve; and while they were eating, he said,

J   **Truly I tell you, one of you will betray me.**

N   And they became greatly distressed and began to say to him one after another,

S   *Surely not I, Lord?*

J   **The one who has dipped his hand into the bowl with me will betray me. The Son of Man goes as it is written of him, but woe to that one by whom the Son of Man is betrayed! It would have been better for that one not to have been born.**

N   Judas, who betrayed him, said,

S   *Surely not I, Rabbi?*

J   **You have said so.**

N   While they were eating, Jesus took a loaf of bread, and after blessing it he broke it, gave it to the disciples, and said,

J   **Take, eat; this is my Body.**

N   Then he took a cup, and after giving thanks he gave it to them, saying,

J   **Drink from it, all of you; for this is my Blood of the covenant, which is poured out for many for the forgiveness of sins. I tell you, I will never again drink of this fruit of the vine until that day when I drink it new with you in my Father's kingdom.**

N   When they had sung the hymn, they went out to the Mount of Olives. Then Jesus said to them,

J   **You will all become deserters because of me this night; for it is written, "I will strike the shepherd, and the sheep of the flock will be scattered." But after I am raised up, I will go ahead of you to Galilee.**

N   Peter said to him,

S   *Though all become deserters because of you, I will never desert you.*

J   **Truly I tell you, this very night, before the cock crows, you will deny me three times.**

N   Peter said to him,

S   *Even though I must die with you, I will not deny you.*

N   And so said all the disciples.

N   Then Jesus went with them to a place called Gethsemane; and he said to his disciples,

J   **Sit here while I go over there and pray.**

N   He took with him Peter and the two sons of Zebedee, and began to be grieved and agitated. Then he said to them,

J   **I am deeply grieved, even to death; remain here, and stay awake with me.**

N   And going a little farther, he threw himself on the ground and prayed,

J   **My Father, if it is possible, let this cup pass from me; yet not what I want, but what you want.**

N   Then he came to the disciples and found them sleeping; and he said to Peter,

J   **So, could you not stay awake with me one hour? Stay awake and pray that you may not come into temptation; for the spirit indeed is willing, but the flesh is weak.**

N   Again he went away for the second time and prayed,

J   **My Father, if this cannot pass unless I drink it, your will be done.**

N   Again he came and found them sleeping, for their eyes were heavy. So leaving them again, he went away and prayed for the third time, saying the same words. Then he came to the disciples and said to them,

J   **Are you still sleeping and taking your rest? See, the hour is at hand, and the Son of Man is betrayed into the hands of sinners. Get up, let us be going. See, my betrayer is at hand.**

N   While he was still speaking, Judas, one of the twelve, arrived; with him was a large crowd with swords and clubs, from the chief priests and the elders of the people. Now the betrayer had given them a sign, saying,

S   *The one I will kiss is the man; arrest him.*

N   At once he came up to Jesus and said,

S   *Greetings, Rabbi!*

N   and kissed him. Jesus said to him,

J   **Friend, do what you are here to do.**

N   Then they came and laid hands on Jesus and arrested him.

Suddenly, one of those with Jesus put his hand on his sword, drew it, and struck the slave of the high priest, cutting off his ear. Then Jesus said to him,

J Put your sword back into its place; for all who take the sword will perish by the sword. Do you think that I cannot appeal to my Father, and he will at once send me more than twelve legions of Angels? But how then would the Scriptures be fulfilled, which say it must happen in this way?

N At that hour Jesus said to the crowds,

J Have you come out with swords and clubs to arrest me as though I were a bandit? Day after day I sat in the temple teaching, and you did not arrest me. But all this has taken place so that the Scriptures of the Prophets may be fulfilled.

N Then all the disciples deserted him and fled.

Those who had arrested Jesus took him to Caiaphas the high priest, in whose house the scribes and the elders had gathered.

But Peter was following him at a distance, as far as the courtyard of the high priest; and going inside, he sat with the guards in order to see how this would end.

Now the chief priests and the whole council were looking for false testimony against Jesus so that they might put him to death, but they found none, though many false witnesses came forward. At last two came forward and said,

S *This fellow said, "I am able to destroy the temple of God and to build it in three days."*

N The high priest stood up and said,

S *Have you no answer? What is it that they testify against you?*

N But Jesus was silent.

Then the high priest said to him,

S *I put you under oath before the living God, tell us if you are the Christ, the Son of God.*

N Jesus said to him,

J You have said so. But I tell you, from now on you will see the Son of Man seated at the right hand of Power and coming on the clouds of heaven.

N   Then the high priest tore his clothes and said,

S   *He has blasphemed! Why do we still need witnesses? You have now heard his blasphemy. What is your verdict?*

N   They answered,

S   *He deserves death.*

N   Then they spat in his face and struck him; and some slapped him, saying,

S   *Prophesy to us, Christ! Who is it that struck you?*

N   Now Peter was sitting outside in the courtyard. A servant girl came to him and said,

S   *You also were with Jesus the Galilean.*

N   But he denied it before all of them, saying,

S   *I do not know what you are talking about.*

N   When Peter went out to the porch, another servant girl saw him, and she said to the bystanders,

S   *This man was with Jesus of Nazareth.*

N   Again he denied it with an oath,

S   *I do not know the man.*

N   After a little while the bystanders came up and said to Peter,

S   *Certainly you are also one of them, for your accent betrays you.*

N   Then he began to curse, and he swore an oath,

S   *I do not know the man!*

N   At that moment the cock crowed. Then Peter remembered what Jesus had said: "Before the cock crows, you will deny me three times." And he went out and wept bitterly.

When morning came, all the chief priests and the elders of the people conferred together against Jesus in order to bring about his death. They bound him, led him away, and handed him over to Pilate the governor.

When Judas, his betrayer, saw that Jesus was condemned, he repented and brought back the thirty pieces of silver to the chief priests and the elders.

S   *I have sinned by betraying innocent blood.*

N   But they said,

S   *What is that to us? See to it yourself.*

N   Throwing down the pieces of silver in the temple, he departed; and he went and hanged himself.

    But the chief priests, taking the pieces of silver, said,

S   *It is not lawful to put them into the treasury, since they are blood money.*

N   After conferring together, they used them to buy the potter's field as a place to bury foreigners. For this reason that field has been called the Field of Blood to this day. Then was fulfilled what had been spoken through the Prophet Jeremiah, "And they took the thirty pieces of silver, the price of the one on whom a price had been set, on whom some of the people of Israel had set a price, and they gave them for the potter's field, as the Lord commanded me."

                                        * * *

N   Now Jesus stood before the governor; and the governor asked him,

S   *Are you the King of the Jews?*

J   **You say so.**

N   But when he was accused by the chief priests and elders, he did not answer. Then Pilate said to him,

S   *Do you not hear how many accusations they make against you?*

N   But Jesus gave him no answer, not even to a single charge, so that the governor was greatly amazed.

    Now at the festival the governor was accustomed to release a prisoner for the crowd, anyone they wanted. At that time they had a notorious prisoner, called Barabbas. So after they had gathered, Pilate said to them,

S   *Whom do you want me to release for you, Barabbas or Jesus who is called the Christ?*

N   For he realized that it was out of jealousy that they had handed him over.

    While he was sitting on the judgment seat, his wife sent word to him,

S   *Have nothing to do with that innocent man, for today I have suffered a great deal because of a dream about him.*

N   Now the chief priests and the elders persuaded the crowds to ask for Barabbas and to have Jesus killed. The governor again said to them,

S   *Which of the two do you want me to release for you?*

N   And they said,

S   *Barabbas.*

N   Pilate said to them,

S   *Then what should I do with Jesus who is called the Christ?*

N   All of them said,

S   *Let him be crucified!*

N   Then he asked,

S   *Why, what evil has he done?*

N   But they shouted all the more,

S   *Let him be crucified!*

N   So when Pilate saw that he could do nothing, but rather that a riot was beginning, he took some water and washed his hands before the crowd, saying,

S   *I am innocent of this man's blood; see to it yourselves.*

N   Then the people as a whole answered,

S   *"His blood be on us and on our children!"*

N   So he released Barabbas for them; and after flogging Jesus, he handed him over to be crucified.

     Then the soldiers of the governor took Jesus into the governor's headquarters, and they gathered the whole cohort around him. They stripped him and put a scarlet robe on him, and after twisting some thorns into a crown, they put it on his head. They put a reed in his right hand and knelt before him and mocked him, saying,

S   *Hail, King of the Jews!*

N   They spat on him, and took the reed and struck him on the head. After mocking him, they stripped him of the robe and put his own clothes on him. Then they led him away to crucify him.

     As they went out, they came upon a man from Cyrene named Simon; they compelled this man to carry his Cross.

And when they came to a place called Golgotha which means Place of a Skull, they offered him wine to drink, mixed with gall; but when he tasted it, he would not drink it.

And when they had crucified him, they divided his clothes among themselves by casting lots; then they sat down there and kept watch over him.

Over his head they put the charge against him, which read, "This is Jesus, the King of the Jews."

Then two bandits were crucified with him, one on his right and one on his left. Those who passed by derided him, shaking their heads and saying,

S   *You who would destroy the temple and build it in three days, save yourself! If you are the Son of God, come down from the Cross.*

N   In the same way the chief priests also, along with the scribes and elders, were mocking him, saying,

S   *He saved others; he cannot save himself. He is the King of Israel; let him come down from the Cross now, and we will believe in him. He trusts in God; let God deliver him now, if he wants to; for he said, "I am God's Son."*

N   The bandits who were crucified with him also taunted him in the same way.

From noon on, darkness came over the whole land until three in the afternoon. And about three o'clock Jesus cried with a loud voice,

J   **Eli, Eli, lema sabachthani?**

N   that is, "My God, my God, why have you forsaken me?" When some of the bystanders heard it, they said,

S   *This man is calling for Elijah.*

N   At once one of them ran and got a sponge, filled it with sour wine, put it on a stick, and gave it to him to drink. But the others said,

S   *Wait, let us see whether Elijah will come to save him.*

N   Then Jesus cried again with a loud voice and breathed his last.

Here all kneel and pause for a short time.

N   At that moment the curtain of the temple was torn in two, from top to bottom. The earth shook, and the rocks were split. The tombs also were opened, and many bodies of the saints who had fallen asleep were raised. After his resurrection they came out of the tombs and entered the holy city and appeared to many.

Now when the centurion and those with him, who were keeping watch over Jesus, saw the earthquake and what took place, they were terrified and said,

S   *Truly this man was God's Son!*

* * *

N   Many women were also there, looking on from a distance; they had followed Jesus from Galilee and had provided for him. Among them were Mary Magdalene, and Mary the mother of James and Joseph, and the mother of the sons of Zebedee.

When it was evening, there came a rich man from Arimathea, named Joseph, who was also a disciple of Jesus. He went to Pilate and asked for the body of Jesus; then Pilate ordered it to be given to him. So Joseph took the body and wrapped it in a clean linen cloth and laid it in his own new tomb, which he had hewn in the rock. He then rolled a great stone to the door of the tomb and went away.

Mary Magdalene and the other Mary were there, sitting opposite the tomb. The next day, that is, after the day of Preparation, the chief priests and the Pharisees gathered before Pilate and said,

S   *Sir, we remember what that impostor said while he was still alive, "After three days I will rise again." Therefore command the tomb to be made secure until the third day; otherwise his disciples may go and steal him away, and tell the people, "He has been raised from the dead," and the last deception would be worse than the first.*

N   Pilate said to them,

S   *You have a guard of soldiers; go, make it as secure as you can.*

N   So they went with the guard and made the tomb secure by sealing the stone.

Holy Week begins on Passion Sunday, which is also called Palm Sunday. On this day we recall Jesus' arrival in Jerusalem, where people greeted him in the streets like a hero, shouting and waving palm branches. During the gospel, we listen to the whole story of Jesus' last days on earth.

Zion was the name of a hill in Jerusalem where the temple was built, but the city itself was often called Zion. Daughter of Zion is another way of naming the entire nation, the whole People of God.

Hosanna is a Hebrew word that means "save us." When the people in Jerusalem shout it as Jesus approaches, they are saying that they know he is the Messiah who has come to save them.

Son of David (or descendant of King David) is a name people used to describe the Messiah who was to come. It is one of the many names given to Jesus in the Bible.

Isaiah was a friend of God who lived about 800 years before Jesus. God chose him to help the people of Israel turn back to God.

The Passion of Jesus is the story of the last hours of his life. It begins with the Last Supper and ends when his body is placed in the tomb. When we speak of the "passion" of Jesus, we mean his suffering.

149

Resurrection of the Lord
Easter Sunday

Peter began to speak: "You know the message that spread throughout Judea, beginning in Galilee after the baptism that John announced: how God anointed Jesus of Nazareth with the Holy Spirit and with power; how he went about doing good and healing all who were oppressed by the devil, for God was with him.

"We are witnesses to all that he did both in Judea and in Jerusalem. They put him to death by hanging him on a tree; but God raised him on the third day and allowed him to appear, not to all the people but to us who were chosen by God as witnesses, and who ate and drank with him after he rose from the dead.

"He commanded us to preach to the people and to testify that he is the one ordained by God as judge of the living and the dead. All the Prophets testify about him that everyone who believes in him receives forgiveness of sins through his name."

The word of the Lord. **Thanks be to God.**

Psalm 118

R. **This is the day the Lord has made;
let us rejoice and be glad.**

or **Alleluia! Alleluia! Alleluia!**

O give thanks to the Lord, for he is good;
his steadfast love endures forever.
Let Israel say,
"His steadfast love endures forever." R.

"The right hand of the Lord is exalted;
the right hand of the Lord does valiantly."
I shall not die, but I shall live,
and recount the deeds of the Lord. R.

The stone that the builders rejected
has become the chief cornerstone.
This is the Lord's doing;
it is marvellous in our eyes. R.

An alternate reading follows.

A reading from the Letter of Saint Paul to the Colossians (3.1-4)

Brothers and sisters: If you have been raised with Christ, seek the things that are above, where Christ is, seated at the right hand of God. Set your minds on things that are above, not on things that are on earth, for you have died, and your life is hidden with Christ in God. When Christ who is your life is revealed, then you also will be revealed with him in glory.

The word of the Lord. **Thanks be to God.**

or

A reading from the first Letter of Saint Paul to the Corinthians (5.6-8)

Do you not know that a little yeast leavens the whole batch of dough? Clean out the old yeast so that you may be a new batch, as you really are unleavened. For our paschal lamb, Christ, has been sacrificed. Therefore, let us celebrate the festival, not with the old yeast, the yeast of malice and evil, but with the unleavened bread of sincerity and truth.

The word of the Lord. **Thanks be to God.**

A reading from the holy Gospel according to John (20.1-18)

The shorter version ends at the asterisks.

Early on the first day of the week, while it was still dark, Mary Magdalene came to the tomb and saw that the stone had been removed from the tomb. So she ran and went to Simon Peter and the other disciple, the one whom Jesus loved, and said to them, "They have taken the Lord out of the tomb, and we do not know where they have laid him."

Then Peter and the other disciple set out and went toward the tomb. The two were running together, but the other disciple outran Peter and reached the tomb first. He bent down to look in and saw the linen wrappings lying there, but he did not go in.

Then Simon Peter came, following him, and went into the tomb. He saw the linen wrappings lying there, and the cloth that had been on Jesus' head, not lying with the linen wrappings but rolled up in a place by itself. Then the other disciple, who reached the tomb first, also went in, and he saw and believed; for as yet they did not understand the Scripture, that he must rise from the dead.

* * *

Then the disciples returned to their homes. But Mary Magdalene stood weeping outside the tomb. As she wept, she bent over to look into the tomb; and she saw two Angels in white, sitting where the body of Jesus had been lying, one at the head and the other at the feet. They said to her, "Woman, why are you weeping?" She said to them, "They have taken away my Lord, and I do not know where they have laid him."

When she had said this, she turned around and saw Jesus standing there, but she did not know that it was Jesus. Jesus said to her, "Woman, why are you weeping? Whom are you looking for?" Supposing him to be the gardener, she said to him, "Sir, if you have carried him away, tell me where you have laid him, and I will take him away."

Jesus said to her, "Mary!" She turned and said to him in Hebrew, "Rabbouni!" which means Teacher. Jesus said to her, "Do not hold on to me, because I have not yet ascended to the Father. But go to my brothers and say to them, 'I am ascending to my Father and your Father, to my God and your God.'"

Mary Magdalene went and announced to the disciples, "I have seen the Lord," and she told them that he had said these things to her.

The Gospel of the Lord.
**Praise to you,
Lord Jesus Christ.**

153

Easter Sunday is the English name for the day Jesus rose from the dead. Easter is an old English word that means 'springtime' and reminds us that we have new life in Jesus' resurrection.

The Acts of the Apostles is a book in the Bible that describes how the Church grew after Jesus rose from the dead. Written by Luke, who also wrote a gospel, it mostly tells the story of Peter and Paul.

Judea was one of three regions in Israel (see the map, page 320). Bethlehem, Jerusalem and Emmaus are some of the cities in Judea.

Although Jesus was born in Bethlehem, he grew up in Nazareth and so was called Jesus of Nazareth. He also began his public life in Nazareth.

Jerusalem is in Judea and is the main city of Israel. Solomon's Temple was built there and Jerusalem was also called the Holy City. Its name means "City of Peace" in Hebrew.

Paul wrote to the Colossians, a Christian community at Colossae in modern-day Turkey, to help them understand that no human powers are greater than Jesus Christ.

John was the other disciple, the one whom Jesus loved. When Jesus was dying on the cross, he asked John to care for his mother, Mary.

2nd Sunday of Easter

They devoted themselves to the Apostles' teaching and fellowship, to the breaking of bread and the prayers. Awe came upon everyone, because many wonders and signs were being done by the Apostles.

All who believed were together and had all things in common; they would sell their possessions and goods and distribute the proceeds to all, as any had need. Day by day, as they spent much time together in the temple, they broke bread in various houses and ate their food with glad and generous hearts, praising God and having the goodwill of all the people. And day by day the Lord added to their number those who were being saved.

The word of the Lord. **Thanks be to God.**

Psalm 118

R̵. **Give thanks to the Lord, for he is good;
his steadfast love endures forever.**

or **Alleluia!**

Let Israel say,
"His steadfast love endures forever."
Let the house of Aaron say,
"His steadfast love endures forever."
Let those who fear the Lord say,
"His steadfast love endures forever." R̵.

I was pushed hard, so that I was falling,
but the Lord helped me.
The Lord is my strength and my might;
he has become my salvation.
There are glad songs of victory
in the tents of the righteous. R̵.

The stone that the builders rejected
has become the chief cornerstone.
This is the Lord's doing;
it is marvellous in our eyes.
This is the day that the Lord has made;
let us rejoice and be glad in it. R̵.

A reading from the first Letter of Saint Peter (1.3-9)

Blessed be the God and Father of our Lord Jesus Christ! By his great mercy he has given us a new birth into a living hope through the resurrection of Jesus Christ from the dead: a birth into an inheritance that is imperishable, undefiled, and unfading, kept in heaven for you, who are being protected by the power of God through faith for a salvation ready to be revealed in the last time.

In this you rejoice, even if now for a little while you have had to suffer various trials, so that the genuineness of your faith—being more precious than gold that, though perishable, is tested by fire—may be found to result in praise and glory and honour when Jesus Christ is revealed.

Although you have not seen him, you love him; and even though you do not see him now, you believe in him and rejoice with an indescribable and glorious joy, for you are receiving the outcome of your faith, the salvation of your souls.

The word of the Lord.
Thanks be to God.

A reading from the holy Gospel according to John (20.19-31)

It was evening on the day Jesus rose from the dead, the first day of the week, and the doors of the house where the disciples had met were locked for fear of the Jews. Jesus came and stood among them and said, "Peace be with you." After he said this, he showed them his hands and his side. Then the disciples rejoiced when they saw the Lord.

Jesus said to them again, "Peace be with you. As the Father has sent me, so I send you."

When he had said this, he breathed on them and said to them, "Receive the Holy Spirit. If you forgive the sins of any, they are forgiven them; if you retain the sins of any, they are retained."

But Thomas, who was called the Twin, one of the twelve, was not with them when Jesus came. So the other disciples told him, "We have seen the Lord." But he said to them, "Unless I see the mark of the nails in his hands, and put my finger in the mark of the nails and my hand in his side, I will not believe."

After eight days his disciples were again in the house, and Thomas was with them. Although the doors were shut, Jesus came and stood among them and said, "Peace be with you." Then he said to Thomas, "Put your finger here and see my hands. Reach out your hand and put it in my side. Do not doubt but believe." Thomas answered him, "My Lord and my God!"

Jesus said to him, "Have you believed because you have seen me? Blessed are those who have not seen and yet have come to believe."

Now Jesus did many other signs in the presence of his disciples, which are not written in this book. But these are written so that you may come to believe that Jesus is the Christ, the Son of God, and that through believing you may have life in his name.

The Gospel of the Lord.
Praise to you, Lord Jesus Christ.

KEY WORDS

Breaking of bread means to celebrate the Lord's supper, as we do at every eucharist.

In the early Christian community, those who believed in Jesus shared all their belongings in common. This way, everyone had all they needed. Today, we can do the same by making sure that no one in our community is in need.

The first Letter of Saint Peter is found in the New Testament. It is a summary of the Good News of Jesus and was written to help the early Christians lead faithful lives.

We rejoice in our salvation, even when life seems difficult. Jesus conquered death by rising from the dead and we know we will see him when he comes again.

The holy Gospel according to John tells us about the life, death and resurrection of Jesus. It was written about 60 years after Jesus died. John's Gospel includes some stories and sayings of Jesus that are not in the other three gospels (Matthew, Mark and Luke).

By showing his hands and his side, Jesus presented the scars left by the nails and the lance that pierced him. It was a way of saying, "It's really me. I was dead, but now I am alive."

When God created the first humans, he breathed life into them. Our life comes from the depths of God's being. When Jesus appeared to his disciples after his death, he also breathed on them, filling them with his Spirit.

3rd Sunday of Easter

When the day of Pentecost had come, Peter, standing with the eleven, raised his voice and addressed the crowd, "Men of Judea and all who live in Jerusalem, let this be known to you, and listen to what I say. Jesus of Nazareth, a man attested to you by God with deeds of power, wonders, and signs that God did through him among you, as you yourselves know—this man, handed over to you according to the definite plan and foreknowledge of God, you crucified and killed by the hands of those outside the law.

"But God raised him up, having freed him from death, because it was impossible for him to be held in its power. For David says concerning him, 'I saw the Lord always before me, for he is at my right hand so that I will not be shaken; therefore my heart was glad, and my tongue rejoiced; moreover my flesh will live in hope. For you will not abandon my soul to Hades, or let your Holy One experience corruption. You have made known to me the ways of life; you will make me full of gladness with your presence.'"

The word of the Lord. **Thanks be to God.**

Psalm 16

R̥. **Lord, you will show me the path of life.**
or **Alleluia!**

Protect me, O God, for in you I take refuge.
I say to the Lord, "You are my Lord;
I have no good apart from you."
The Lord is my chosen portion and my cup;
    you hold my lot. R̥.

I bless the Lord who gives me counsel;
in the night also my heart instructs me.
I keep the Lord always before me;
    because he is at my right hand, I shall not be moved. R̥.

Therefore my heart is glad, and my soul rejoices;
my body also rests secure.
For you do not give me up to Sheol,
    or let your faithful one see the Pit. R̥.

You show me the path of life.
In your presence there is fullness of joy;
    in your right hand are pleasures forevermore. R̥.

A reading from the first Letter of Saint Peter
(1.17-21)

Beloved: If you invoke as Father the one who judges each person impartially according to each one's deeds, live in reverent fear during the time of your exile.

You know that you were ransomed from the futile ways inherited from your ancestors, not with perishable things like silver or gold, but with the precious blood of Christ, like that of a lamb without defect or blemish.

Christ was destined before the foundation of the world, but was revealed at the end of the ages for your sake. Through him you have come to trust in God, who raised him from the dead and gave him glory, so that your faith and hope are set on God.

The word of the Lord. **Thanks be to God.**

A reading from the holy Gospel according to Luke
(24.13-35)

On the first day of the week, two of the disciples were going to a village called Emmaus, about eleven kilometres from Jerusalem, and talking with each other about all these things that had happened. While they were talking and discussing, Jesus himself came near and went with them, but their eyes were kept from recognizing him.

And he said to them, "What are you discussing with each other while you walk along?" They stood still, looking sad. Then one of them, whose name was Cleopas, answered him, "Are you the only stranger in Jerusalem who does not know the things that have taken place there in these days?"

He asked them, "What things?" They replied, "The things about Jesus of Nazareth, who was a Prophet mighty in deed and word before God and all the people, and how our chief priests and leaders handed him over to be condemned to death and crucified him. But we had hoped that he was the one to redeem Israel. Yes, and besides all this, it is now the third day since these things took place. Moreover, some women of our group astounded us. They were at the tomb early this morning, and when they did not find his body there, they came back and told us that they had indeed seen a vision of Angels who said that he was alive. Some of those who were with us went to the tomb and found it just as the women had said; but they did not see him."

Then he said to them, "Oh, how foolish you are, and how slow of heart to believe all that the Prophets have declared! Was it not necessary that the Christ should suffer these things and then enter into his glory?"

Then beginning with Moses and all the Prophets, he interpreted to them the things about himself in all the Scriptures. As they came near the village to which they were going, he walked ahead as if he were going on. But they urged him strongly, saying, "Stay with us, because it is almost evening and the day is now nearly over." So he went in to stay with them.

When he was at the table with them, he took bread, blessed and broke it, and gave it to them. Then their eyes were opened, and they recognized him; and he vanished from their sight.

They said to each other, "Were not our hearts burning within us while he was talking to us on the road, while he was opening the Scriptures to us?"

That same hour they got up and returned to Jerusalem; and they found the eleven and their companions gathered together. These were saying, "The Lord has risen indeed, and he has appeared to Simon!"

Then they told what had happened on the road, and how he had been made known to them in the breaking of the bread.

The Gospel of the Lord.
Praise to you,
Lord Jesus Christ.

Pentecost is the Greek word for a Jewish festival that takes place on the fiftieth day after Passover. For Christians, Pentecost is the feast of the coming of the Holy Spirit (see page 183).

David was the second king of Israel. He lived about 1,000 years before Christ. David is considered to be the author of the 150 psalms. In this passage from Acts, Peter is quoting from Psalm 16.

If we have reverent fear for someone, we are not afraid because they are frightening. Instead, we are filled with awe because of their greatness, and we try to honour them with our lives.

Jewish people made sacrifices of animals to God. Because Jesus' sacrifice brought us back to God, the Bible compares Jesus to a lamb, one without any stain.

The holy Gospel according to Luke was written for people who, like Luke, weren't Jewish before becoming Christian. This gospel tells the most about Mary, the mother of Jesus.

The Scriptures are the written word of God. We read them in the Bible.

Jesus' disciples recognized him in the breaking of the bread, because Jesus had done the same thing at many meals, especially the Last Supper. Jesus said to do this in his memory, and we remember Jesus as our living bread when we celebrate the eucharist.

4th Sunday of Easter

When the day of Pentecost had come, Peter, standing with the eleven, raised his voice and addressed the crowd. "Let the entire house of Israel know with certainty that God has made him both Lord and Christ, this Jesus whom you crucified."

Now when the people heard this, they were cut to the heart and said to Peter and to the other Apostles, "Brothers, what should we do?" Peter said to them, "Repent, and be baptized every one of you in the name of Jesus Christ so that your sins may be forgiven; and you will receive the gift of the Holy Spirit. For the promise is for you, for your children, and for all who are far away, everyone whom the Lord our God calls to him."

And he testified with many other arguments and exhorted them, saying, "Save yourselves from this corrupt generation." So those who welcomed his message were baptized, and that day were added about three thousand souls.

The word of the Lord. **Thanks be to God.**

Psalm 23

R. **The Lord is my shepherd; I shall not want.**
or **Alleluia!**

The Lord is my shepherd, I shall not want.
He makes me lie down in green pastures;
he leads me beside still waters;
he restores my soul. R.

He leads me in right paths for his name's sake.
Even though I walk through the darkest valley,
    I fear no evil;
for you are with me;
your rod and your staff—they comfort me. R.

You prepare a table before me
in the presence of my enemies;
you anoint my head with oil;
my cup overflows. R.

Surely goodness and mercy shall follow me
all the days of my life,
and I shall dwell in the house of the Lord
my whole life long. R.

A reading from the first Letter of Saint Peter
(2.20-25)

Beloved: If you endure when you do right and suffer for it, you have God's approval. For to this you have been called, because Christ also suffered for you, leaving you an example, so that you should follow in his steps. "He committed no sin, and no deceit was found in his mouth." When he was abused, he did not return abuse; when he suffered, he did not threaten; but he entrusted himself to the one who judges justly.

Christ himself bore our sins in his body on the Cross, so that, free from sins, we might live for righteousness; by his wounds you have been healed. For you were going astray like sheep, but now you have returned to the shepherd and guardian of your souls.

The word of the Lord. **Thanks be to God.**

A reading from the holy Gospel according to John
(10.1-10)

Jesus said: "Very truly, I tell you, anyone who does not enter the sheepfold by the gate but climbs in by another way is a thief and a bandit. The one who enters by the gate is the shepherd of the sheep. The gatekeeper opens the gate for him, and the sheep hear his voice. He calls his own sheep by name and leads them out. When he has brought out all his own, he goes ahead of them, and the sheep follow him because they know his voice. They will not follow a stranger, but they will run from him because they do not know the voice of strangers."

Jesus used this figure of speech with them, but they did not understand what he was saying to them. So again Jesus said to them, "Very truly, I tell you, I am the gate for the sheep. All who came before me are thieves and bandits; but the sheep did not listen to them. I am the gate. Whoever enters by me will be saved, and will come in and go out and find pasture. The thief comes only to steal and kill and destroy. I came that they may have life, and have it abundantly."

The Gospel of the Lord. **Praise to you, Lord Jesus Christ.**

The eleven are the disciples of Jesus. They were twelve at first, but Judas Iscariot, who betrayed Jesus, left before Jesus died.

To repent means to be sorry for doing something wrong and to change our behaviour for the better.

When Peter says that God's promises are for everyone, he is saying something new. He means that God's promises are not just for the People of Israel, but for all people everywhere. This is the New Covenant.

A shepherd is someone who takes care of a flock of sheep. He would spend days or weeks with his flock, sleeping with them and making sure they were always safe. God loves us with the same constant care.

The sheepfold is a fenced-in area for sheep. It helps keep them safe from other animals that might attack them.

When we have life abundantly, it means our hearts are full of joy and peace. We live our lives wanting to help others because of our friendship with Jesus.

5th Sunday of Easter

Now during those days, when the disciples were increasing in number, the Hellenists complained against the Hebrews because their widows were being neglected in the daily distribution of food. And the twelve called together the whole community of the disciples and said, "It is not right that we should neglect the word of God in order to wait on tables. Therefore, brothers, select from among yourselves seven men of good standing, full of the Spirit and of wisdom, whom we may appoint to this task, while we, for our part, will devote ourselves to prayer and to serving the word."

What they said pleased the whole community, and they chose Stephen, a man full of faith and the Holy Spirit, together with Philip, Prochorus, Nicanor, Timon, Parmenas, and Nicolaus, a convert of Antioch. They had these men stand before the Apostles, who prayed and laid their hands on them.

The word of God continued to spread; the number of the disciples increased greatly in Jerusalem, and a great many of the priests became obedient to the faith.

The word of the Lord. **Thanks be to God.**

Psalm 33

℞ Let your love be upon us, Lord, even as we hope in you.
or **Alleluia!**

Rejoice in the Lord, O you righteous.
Praise befits the upright.
Praise the Lord with the lyre;
make melody to him with the harp of ten strings. ℞

For the word of the Lord is upright,
and all his work is done in faithfulness.
He loves righteousness and justice;
he earth is full of the steadfast love of the Lord. ℞

Truly the eye of the Lord is on those who fear him,
on those who hope in his steadfast love,
to deliver their soul from death,
and to keep them alive in famine. ℞

Beloved: Come to the Lord, a living stone, though rejected by human beings yet chosen and precious in God's sight. Like living stones, let yourselves be built into a spiritual house, to be a holy priesthood, to offer spiritual sacrifices acceptable to God through Jesus Christ.

For it stands in Scripture: "See, I am laying in Zion a stone, a cornerstone chosen and precious; and whoever believes in him will not be put to shame." To you then who believe, he is precious; but for those who do not believe, "The stone that the builders rejected has become the very head of the corner," and "A stone that makes them stumble, and a rock that makes them fall." They stumble because they disobey the word, as they were destined to do.

But you are a chosen race, a royal priesthood, a holy nation, God's own people, in order that you may proclaim the mighty acts of him who called you out of darkness into his marvellous light.

The word of the Lord. **Thanks be to God.**

Jesus said to his disciples: "Do not let your hearts be troubled. Believe in God, believe also in me. In my Father's house there are many dwelling places. If it were not so, would I have told you that I go to prepare a place for you? And if I go and prepare a place for you, I will come again and will take you to myself, so that where I am, there you may be also. And you know the way to the place where I am going."

Thomas said to him, "Lord, we do not know where you are going. How can we know the way?"

Jesus said to him, "I am the way, and the truth, and the life. No one comes to the Father except through me. If you know me, you will know my Father also. From now on you do know him and have seen him."

Philip said to him, "Lord, show us the Father, and we will be satisfied." Jesus said to him, "Have I been with you all this time,

Philip, and you still do not know me? Whoever has seen me has seen the Father. How can you say, 'Show us the Father'? Do you not believe that I am in the Father and the Father is in me? The words that I say to you I do not speak on my own; but the Father who dwells in me does his works. Believe me that I am in the Father and the Father is in me; but if you do not, then believe me because of the works themselves. Very truly, I tell you, the one who believes in me will also do the works that I do and, in fact, will do greater works than these, because I am going to the Father."

The Gospel of the Lord. **Praise to you, Lord Jesus Christ.**

KEY WORDS

The word of God is the Good News—Jesus is the Saviour of the world! The disciples were worried that people were getting too busy and were not spending time praying and sharing this Good News. So they named some people to devote themselves especially to the word of God.

Stephen was one of the first ministers in the early Church. He did much good work. Stephen was killed because of his faith in Jesus and was the first martyr. The feast of Stephen is December 26.

The disciples laid their hands on the heads of others as a form of prayer. It was also a way of sending someone off to do a task. This gesture is now part of certain sacraments, such as confirmation and holy orders (priesthood). It is a sign that the power of God, the Holy Spirit, is being given to the person.

When Peter calls us living stones, he is telling us that we are a very important part of the Church. If we do not all stand together, the Church will lose its strength.

Through our baptism, all Christians share in the holy priesthood of Jesus: we offer our lives to God and rejoice in his love. Some Christians are specially anointed as priests to preside at eucharist and be leaders of the community.

God's people are a chosen race—from generation to generation, throughout the ages—just like a family.

When Jesus says that he will "take you to myself," he is making a beautiful promise. Jesus takes us into his heart.

6th Sunday of Easter

In those days: Philip went down to the city of Samaria and proclaimed the Christ to them. The crowds with one accord listened eagerly to what was said by Philip, hearing and seeing the signs that he did, for unclean spirits, crying with loud shrieks, came out of many who were possessed; and many others who were paralysed or lame were cured. So there was great joy in that city.

Now when the Apostles at Jerusalem heard that Samaria had accepted the word of God, they sent Peter and John to them. The two went down and prayed for them that they might receive the Holy Spirit; (for as yet the Spirit had not come upon any of them; they had only been baptized in the name of the Lord Jesus). Then Peter and John laid their hands on them, and they received the Holy Spirit.

The word of the Lord. **Thanks be to God.**

Psalm 66

R. **Make a joyful noise to God, all the earth!**
or **Alleluia!**

Make a joyful noise to God, all the earth!
sing the glory of his name;
give to him glorious praise.
Say to God, "How awesome are your deeds!" R.

"All the earth worships you;
they sing praises to you, sing praises to your name."
Come and see what God has done:
he is awesome in his deeds among the children of Adam. R.

He turned the sea into dry land;
they passed through the river on foot.
There we rejoiced in him,
who rules by his might forever. R.

Come and hear, all you who fear God,
and I will tell what he has done for me.
Blessed be God, because he has not rejected my prayer
or removed his steadfast love from me. R.

A reading from the first Letter of Saint Peter (3.15-18)

Beloved: In your hearts sanctify Christ as Lord. Always be ready to make your defence to anyone who demands from you an accounting for the hope that is in you; yet do it with gentleness and reverence. Keep your conscience clear, so that, when you are maligned, those who abuse you for your good conduct in Christ may be put to shame. For it is better to suffer for doing good, if suffering should be God's will, than to suffer for doing evil.

For Christ also suffered for sins once for all, the righteous for the unrighteous, in order to bring you to God. He was put to death in the flesh, but made alive in the spirit.

The word of the Lord. **Thanks be to God.**

A reading from the holy Gospel according to John (14.15-21)

Jesus said to his disciples: "If you love me, you will keep my commandments. And I will ask the Father, and he will give you another Advocate, to be with you forever. This is the Spirit of truth, whom the world cannot receive, because it neither sees him nor knows him. You know him, because he abides with you, and he will be in you.

"I will not leave you orphaned; I am coming to you. In a little while the world will no longer see me, but you will see me; because I live, you also will live. On that day you will know that I am in my Father, and you in me, and I in you.

"The one who has my commandments and keeps them is the one who loves me; and the one who loves me will be loved by my Father, and I will love them and reveal myself to them."

The Gospel of the Lord. **Praise to you, Lord Jesus Christ.**

Philip in today's reading is not Philip the apostle, but one of the seven deacons named by the apostles to care for widows and the poor. He was mentioned last Sunday, along with Stephen, the first martyr.

Before Jesus went to heaven, he said not to be afraid, because he would send the Holy Spirit to help us remember all that Jesus taught. The Holy Spirit came upon the early Church at Pentecost.

To sanctify something is to make it holy. When we carry the Holy Spirit in our hearts, and try to love each other, we proclaim that Jesus is holy.

Christ is a Greek word that means 'anointed.' The chosen person was blessed with holy oil and given a special mission. The Aramaic word for 'anointed' is 'Messiah.'

The Advocate is another name for the Holy Spirit, sent by Jesus to be our helper and guide until the end of time.

The Holy Spirit abides or lives in us. The Spirit encourages us and gives us the words we need to speak about our faith in Jesus Christ.

When Jesus speaks of "the one who loves me," he means those who show their love of God by their loving actions. Love is more than a good feeling—it is as way of life.

Ascension of the Lord

In the first book, Theophilus, I wrote about all that Jesus did and taught from the beginning until the day when he was taken up to heaven, after giving instructions through the Holy Spirit to the Apostles whom he had chosen. After his suffering he presented himself alive to them by many convincing proofs, appearing to them during forty days and speaking about the kingdom of God.

While staying with them, he ordered them not to leave Jerusalem, but to wait there for the promise of the Father. "This," he said, "is what you have heard from me; for John baptized with water, but you will be baptized with the Holy Spirit not many days from now."

So when they had come together, they asked him, "Lord, is this the time when you will restore the kingdom to Israel?" He replied, "It is not for you to know the times or periods that the Father has set by his own authority. But you will receive power when the Holy Spirit has come upon you; and you will be my witnesses in Jerusalem, in all Judea and Samaria, and to the ends of the earth."

When he had said this, as they were watching, he was lifted up, and a cloud took him out of their sight. While he was going and they were gazing up toward heaven, suddenly two men in white robes stood by them. They said, "Men of Galilee, why do you stand looking up toward heaven? This Jesus, who has been taken up from you into heaven, will come in the same way as you saw him go into heaven."

The word of the Lord. **Thanks be to God.**

R. **God has gone up with a shout,**
the Lord with the sound of a trumpet.
or **Alleluia!**

Clap your hands, all you peoples;
shout to God with loud songs of joy.
For the Lord, the Most High, is awesome,
a great king over all the earth. R.

God has gone up with a shout,
the Lord with the sound of a trumpet.
Sing praises to God, sing praises;
sing praises to our King, sing praises. R.

For God is the king of all the earth;
sing praises with a Psalm.
God is king over the nations;
God sits on his holy throne. R.

A reading from the Letter of Saint Paul to the Ephesians (1.17-23)

Brothers and sisters: I pray that the God of our Lord Jesus Christ, the Father of glory, may give you a spirit of wisdom and revelation as you come to know him, so that, with the eyes of your heart enlightened, you may know what is the hope to which he has called you, what are the riches of his glorious inheritance among the saints, and what is the immeasurable greatness of his power for us who believe, according to the working of his great power.

God put this power to work in Christ when he raised him from the dead and seated him at his right hand in the heavenly places, far above all rule and authority and power and dominion, and above every name that is named, not only in this age but also in the age to come.

And he has put all things under his feet and has made him the head over all things for the Church, which is his body, the fullness of him who fills all in all.

The word of the Lord. **Thanks be to God.**

The eleven disciples went to Galilee, to the mountain to which Jesus had directed them. When they saw him, they worshipped him; but some doubted.

And Jesus came and said to them, "All authority in heaven and on earth has been given to me. Go therefore and make disciples of all nations, baptizing them in the name of the Father and of the Son and of the Holy Spirit, and teaching them to obey everything that I have commanded you. And remember, I am with you always, to the end of the age."

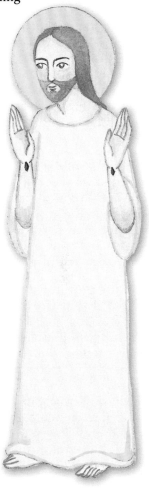

The Gospel of the Lord.
Praise to you, Lord Jesus Christ.

On the feast of the Ascension, we remember the moment when Jesus returns to the house of his Father, forty days after rising from the dead. Jesus no longer appears to his disciples, but he sends the Holy Spirit at Pentecost.

Theophilus (a Greek name that means "friend of God") lived in Antioch. He was a leader of the Christian communities of Greece. Luke sent his Gospel as well as the Acts of the Apostles to him.

In the days of Jesus, Israel was part of the Roman Empire and was not free to govern itself. Some of the disciples hoped that Jesus would free Israel from Rome's bitter rule and bring back the ancient kingdom of Israel.

Galilee is a province in the north of Palestine (see the map, page 320). Nazareth, the town where Jesus lived with his parents, is in Galilee. So is the Sea of Tiberias, where some of Jesus' disciples worked as fishermen. In Jerusalem, to the south, Jesus and his followers were recognized as Galileans because of their accent.

Sitting at the right hand of God is a way of saying that Jesus is very close to God the Father.

When Paul speaks of all rule and authority and power and dominion, he is not talking about earthly governments. Instead, he means different kinds of angels in heaven. Jesus sits so close to the Father in heaven that he is above all the angels.

"I am with you" is the promise Jesus made to us. He is with us when we gather in his name as a community, when we listen to God's word, when we celebrate the eucharist, and when we share his love with others.

Pentecost Sunday

When the day of Pentecost had come, they were all together in one place. And suddenly from heaven there came a sound like the rush of a violent wind, and it filled the entire house where they were sitting. Divided tongues, as of fire, appeared among them, and a tongue rested on each of them. All of them were filled with the Holy Spirit and began to speak in other languages, as the Spirit gave them ability.

Now there were devout Jews from every nation under heaven living in Jerusalem. And at this sound the crowd gathered and was bewildered, because each one heard them speaking in their own language. Amazed and astonished, they asked, "Are not all these who are speaking Galileans? And how is it that we hear, each of us, in our own language? Parthians, Medes, Elamites, and residents of Mesopotamia, Judea and Cappadocia, Pontus and Asia, Phrygia and Pamphylia, Egypt and the parts of Libya belonging to Cyrene, and visitors from Rome, both Jews and converts, Cretans and Arabs—in our own languages we hear them speaking about God's deeds of power."

The word of the Lord. **Thanks be to God.**

Psalm 104

R. **Lord, send forth your Spirit,**
and renew the face of the earth.

or **Alleluia!**

Bless the Lord, O my soul.
O Lord my God, you are very great.
O Lord, how manifold are your works!
The earth is full of your creatures. R.

When you take away their breath,
they die and return to their dust.
When you send forth your spirit, they are created;
and you renew the face of the earth. R.

May the glory of the Lord endure forever;
may the Lord rejoice in his works.
May my meditation be pleasing to him,
for I rejoice in the Lord. R.

Brothers and sisters: No one can say "Jesus is Lord" except by the Holy Spirit.

Now there are varieties of gifts, but the same Spirit; and there are varieties of services, but the same Lord; and there are varieties of activities, but it is the same God who activates all of them in everyone. To each is given the manifestation of the Spirit for the common good.

For just as the body is one and has many members, and all the members of the body, though many, are one body, so it is with Christ. For in the one Spirit we were all baptized into one body—Jews or Greeks, slaves or free—and we were all made to drink of one Spirit.

The word of the Lord. **Thanks be to God.**

It was evening on the day Jesus rose from the dead, the first day of the week, and the doors of the house where the disciples had met were locked for fear of the Jews. Jesus came and stood among them and said, "Peace be with you." After he said this, he showed them his hands and his side. Then the disciples rejoiced when they saw the Lord.

Jesus said to them again, "Peace be with you. As the Father has sent me, so I send you."

When he had said this, he breathed on them and said to them, "Receive the Holy Spirit. If you forgive the sins of any, they are forgiven them; if you retain the sins of any, they are retained."

The Gospel of the Lord. **Praise to you, Lord Jesus Christ.**

God's deeds of power are so great that they cannot be counted, but the greatest of these is that he sent his Son to save us. The disciples proclaimed God's marvellous deed—the death and resurrection of Jesus.

The Corinthians were a community of Christians who lived in Corinth, a city in Greece. Paul wrote them several letters, two of which are in the Bible.

In the Bible, God is called the Lord because God is more powerful than all human power.

Paul compares the Church to a human body. Although all the parts are different, each is important and all the parts together make one complete body.

We know Jesus is with us when we have peace in our home, our school, our community and our country. If we don't have this peace, then we must change the way we are living.

Jesus gave his disciples an important power—to forgive the sins of others. We promise to do the same each time we pray the Lord's Prayer ("Our Father...").

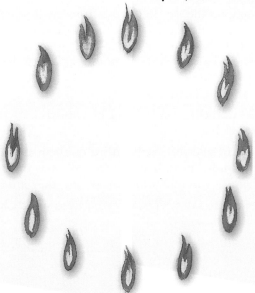

Solemnity of
the Most Holy Trinity

Moses rose early in the morning and went up on Mount Sinai, as the Lord had commanded him, and took in his hand the two tablets of stone. The Lord descended in the cloud and stood with him there, and proclaimed the name, "The Lord."

The Lord passed before Moses, and proclaimed, "The Lord, the Lord, a God merciful and gracious, slow to anger, and abounding in steadfast love and faithfulness."

And Moses quickly bowed his head toward the earth, and worshipped. He said, "If now I have found favour in your sight, O Lord, I pray, let the Lord go with us. Although this is a stiff-necked people, pardon our iniquity and our sin, and take us for your inheritance."

The word of the Lord. **Thanks be to God.**

Daniel 3

R̰ **Glory and praise for ever!**

Blessed are you, O Lord, God of our fathers
and blessed is your glorious and holy name. R̰

Blessed are you in the temple of your holy glory,
and to be extolled and highly glorified forever. R̰

Blessed are you on the throne of your kingdom,
and to be extolled and highly exalted forever. R̰

Blessed are you who look into the depths
from your throne on the cherubim. R̰

Blessed are you in the firmament of heaven,
to be sung and glorified forever. R̰

A reading from the second Letter of Saint Paul to the Corinthians (13.11-13)

Brothers and sisters, put things in order, listen to my appeal, agree with one another, live in peace; and the God of love and peace will be with you. Greet one another with a holy kiss. All the saints greet you.

The grace of the Lord Jesus Christ, the love of God, and the communion of the Holy Spirit be with all of you.

The word of the Lord. **Thanks be to God.**

A reading from the holy Gospel according to John (3.16-18)

Jesus said to Nicodemus: "God so loved the world that he gave his only-begotten Son, so that everyone who believes in him may not perish but may have eternal life.

"Indeed, God did not send the Son into the world to condemn the world, but in order that the world might be saved through him. The one who believes in him is not condemned; but the one who does not believe is condemned already, for not having believed in the name of the only-begotten Son of God."

The Gospel of the Lord. **Praise to you, Lord Jesus Christ.**

GENINA

Mount Sinai was a place where God often visited his people. God spoke to Moses on Mount Sinai and gave him the Ten Commandments. Mount Sinai was also called Mount Horeb.

Even today we might inscribe important things in stone. We do this so that the words will not be erased or forgotten. When God spoke to Moses on Mount Sinai, God ordered him to write the Ten Commandments on two tablets of stone.

Saying "Blessed are you, O Lord" is a way of praising God. We are saying, "Let the whole world know how great and wonderful God is!"

The phrase brothers and sisters is used often in the New Testament and in the Church today. Jesus called the apostles his brothers and the early Christians also called each other brother and sister. This shows that we are members of one family because we share the same Father.

To perish is to die. Jesus promises that those who believe in him will not perish forever. Jesus promises us eternal life with God, and even though we will die, we already enjoy our new life with God.

Solemnity of the Most Holy Body and Blood of Christ

Moses spoke to the people: "Remember the long way that the Lord your God has led you these forty years in the wilderness, in order to humble you, testing you to know what was in your heart, whether or not you would keep his commandments. He humbled you by letting you hunger, then by feeding you with manna, with which neither you nor your ancestors were acquainted, in order to make you understand that man does not live by bread alone, but by every word that comes from the mouth of the Lord.

"Do not exalt yourself, forgetting the Lord your God, who brought you out of the land of Egypt, out of the house of slavery, who led you through the great and terrible wilderness, an arid wasteland with poisonous snakes and scorpions. He made water flow for you from flint rock, and fed you in the wilderness with manna that your ancestors did not know, to humble you and to test you, and in the end to do you good."

The word of the Lord. **Thanks be to God.**

Psalm 147

R. **Praise the Lord, Jerusalem.**
or **Alleluia!**

Praise the Lord, O Jerusalem!
Praise your God, O Zion!
For he strengthens the bars of your gates;
he blesses your children within you. R.

He grants peace within your borders;
he fills you with the finest of wheat.
He sends out his command to the earth;
his word runs swiftly. R.

He declares his word to Jacob,
his statutes and ordinances to Israel.
He has not dealt thus with any other nation;
they do not know his ordinances. R.

A reading from the first Letter of Saint Paul to the Corinthians (10.16-17)

Brothers and sisters: The cup of blessing that we bless, is it not a sharing in the Blood of Christ? The bread that we break, is it not a sharing in the Body of Christ?

Because there is one bread, we who are many are one body, for we all partake of the one bread.

The word of the Lord. **Thanks be to God.**

A reading from the holy Gospel according to John (6.51-59)

Jesus said to the people: "I am the living bread that came down from heaven. Whoever eats of this bread will live forever; and the bread that I will give for the life of the world is my flesh."

The people then disputed among themselves, saying, "How can this man give us his flesh to eat?"

So Jesus said to them, "Very truly, I tell you, unless you eat the flesh of the Son of Man and drink his blood, you have no life in you. Whoever eats my flesh and drinks my blood has eternal life, and I will raise them up on the last day; for my flesh is true food and my blood is true drink. Whoever eats my flesh and drinks my blood abides in me, and I in them.

"Just as the living Father sent me, and I live because of the Father, so whoever eats me will live because of me. This is the bread that came down from heaven, not like that which your ancestors ate, and they died. But the one who eats this bread will live forever."

Jesus said these things while he was teaching in the synagogue at Capernaum.

The Gospel of the Lord. **Praise to you, Lord Jesus Christ.**

The commandments help us love God and all the people we meet along the road of life.

Manna is a food that God sent to the Israelites when they were crossing the desert and had nothing to eat. Manna was like bread falling from heaven.

The holy Gospel according to John tells us about the life, death and resurrection of Jesus. It was written about 60 years after Jesus died. John's Gospel includes some stories and sayings of Jesus that are not in the other three gospels (Matthew, Mark and Luke).

The people who lived before us, our ancestors, left slavery in Egypt 1,000 years before Christ was born. They wandered in the desert for 40 years before coming to the Promised Land. When they were hungry, God sent them manna from heaven. God sent his son, Jesus, to be our living bread. God always takes care of his people!

14th Sunday in Ordinary Time

Thus says the Lord:
Rejoice greatly, O daughter Zion!
Shout aloud, O daughter Jerusalem!
Lo, your king comes to you;
triumphant and victorious is he,
humble and riding on a donkey,
on a colt, the foal of a donkey.

He will cut off the chariot from Ephraim
and the war horse from Jerusalem;
and the warrior's bow shall be cut off,
and he shall command peace to the nations;
his dominion shall be from sea to sea,
and from the River to the ends of the earth.

The word of the Lord. **Thanks be to God.**

Psalm 145

R. **I will bless your name for ever, my King and my God.**
or **Alleluia!**

I will extol you, my God and King,
and bless your name forever and ever.
Every day I will bless you,
and praise your name forever and ever. R.

The Lord is gracious and merciful,
slow to anger and abounding in steadfast love.
The Lord is good to all,
and his compassion is over all that he has made. R.

All your works shall give thanks to you, O Lord,
and all your faithful shall bless you.
They shall speak of the glory of your kingdom,
and tell of your power. R.

The Lord is faithful in all his words,
and gracious in all his deeds.
The Lord upholds all who are falling,
and raises up all who are bowed down. R.

Brothers and sisters: You are not in the flesh; you are in the Spirit, since the Spirit of God dwells in you. Anyone who does not have the Spirit of Christ does not belong to him.

If the Spirit of God who raised Jesus from the dead dwells in you, he who raised Christ from the dead will give life to your mortal bodies also through his Spirit that dwells in you.

So then, brothers and sisters, we are debtors, not to the flesh, to live according to the flesh—for if you live according to the flesh, you will die; but if by the Spirit you put to death the deeds of the body, you will live.

The word of the Lord. **Thanks be to God.**

At that time Jesus said, "I thank you, Father, Lord of heaven and earth, because you have hidden these things from the wise and the intelligent and have revealed them to infants; yes, Father, for such was your gracious will."

He continued: "All things have been handed over to me by my Father; and no one knows the Son except the Father, and no one knows the Father except the Son and anyone to whom the Son chooses to reveal him.

"Come to me, all you that are weary and are carrying heavy burdens, and I will give you rest. Take my yoke upon you, and learn from me; for I am gentle and humble in heart, and you will find rest for your souls. For my yoke is easy, and my burden is light."

The Gospel of the Lord.
Praise to you, Lord Jesus Christ.

Zechariah was a prophet who lived 520 years before Christ. The temple in Jerusalem had been destroyed by Nebuchadnezzar, and Zechariah was trying to lift the spirits of the people of Israel. A good part of the book of Zechariah is dedicated to announcing the coming of the Messiah. He will come like a king, like a shepherd, or like the servant of the Lord.

Zion was the name of a hill in Jerusalem where the temple was built, but the city itself was often called Zion. Daughter Zion is another way of naming the entire nation, the whole People of God.

Ephraim is the name of one of Jacob's sons and one of the twelve tribes of Israel. The Bible sometimes uses this name for the whole people of Israel.

The Spirit of God speaks in our hearts and leads us to follow Jesus by our words and actions. If we listen to the Spirit and follow where it leads, we are living according to the Spirit.

The gospel is the message of Jesus. It comes from an old English word 'godspel' that means "good news."

Everyone has burdens to carry in life—times of pain or suffering. But if we live as Jesus taught us, we will also have great joy and the hard times will be easier to bear. Jesus brings us true consolation and comfort.

15th Sunday in Ordinary Time

A reading from the book of the Prophet Isaiah

(55.10-11)

Thus says the Lord: "As the rain and the snow come down from heaven, and do not return there until they have watered the earth, making it bring forth and sprout, giving seed to the sower and bread to the one who eats, so shall my word be that goes out from my mouth; it shall not return to me empty, but it shall accomplish that which I purpose, and succeed in the thing for which I sent it."

The word of the Lord. **Thanks be to God.**

Psalm 65

R. **The seed that fell on good soil produced a hundredfold.**

You visit the earth and water it,
you greatly enrich it;
the river of God is full of water;
you provide the people with grain. R.

For so you have prepared the earth:
you water its furrows abundantly,
settling its ridges, softening it with showers,
and blessing its growth. R.

You crown the year with your bounty;
your pathways overflow with richness.
The pastures of the wilderness overflow,
the hills gird themselves with joy. R.

The meadows clothe themselves with flocks,
the valleys deck themselves with grain,
they shout and sing together for joy. R.

Brothers and sisters: I consider that the sufferings of this present time are not worth comparing with the glory about to be revealed to us. For the creation waits with eager longing for the revealing of the children of God; for the creation was subjected to futility, not of its own will but by the will of the one who subjected it, in hope that the creation itself will be set free from its bondage to decay and will obtain the freedom of the glory of the children of God.

We know that the whole creation has been groaning in labour pains until now; and not only the creation, but we ourselves, who have the first fruits of the Spirit, groan inwardly while we wait for adoption to sonship, the redemption of our bodies.

The word of the Lord. **Thanks be to God.**

The shorter reading ends at the asterisks.

Jesus went out of the house and sat beside the sea. Such great crowds gathered around him that he got into a boat and sat there, while the whole crowd stood on the beach. And he told them many things in parables.

"Listen! A sower went out to sow. And as he sowed, some seeds fell on the path, and the birds came and ate them up. Other seeds fell on rocky ground, where they did not have much soil, and they sprang up quickly, since they had no depth of soil. But when the sun rose, they were scorched; and since they had no root, they withered away. Other seeds fell among thorns, and the thorns grew up and choked them. Other seeds fell on good soil and brought forth grain, some a hundredfold, some sixty, some thirty. Let anyone with ears listen!"

* * *

Then the disciples came and asked Jesus, "Why do you speak to them in parables?" He answered, "To you it has been given to know the secrets of the kingdom of heaven, but to them it has not been given. For to those who have, more will be given, and they will have an abundance; but from those who have nothing, even what they have will be taken away.

"The reason I speak to them in parables is that 'seeing they do not perceive, and hearing they do not listen, nor do they understand.' With them indeed is fulfilled the prophecy of Isaiah that says: 'You will indeed listen, but never understand, and you will indeed look, but never perceive. For this people's heart has grown dull, and their ears are hard of hearing, and they have shut their eyes; so that they might not look with their eyes, and listen with their ears, and understand with their heart and turn —and I would heal them.'

"But blessed are your eyes, for they see, and your ears, for they hear. Truly I tell you, many Prophets and righteous people longed to see what you see, but did not see it, and to hear what you hear, but did not hear it.

"Hear then the parable of the sower. When anyone hears the word of the kingdom and does not understand it, the evil one comes and snatches away what is sown in the heart; this is what was sown on the path. As for what was sown on rocky ground, this is the one who hears the word and immediately receives it with joy; yet such a person has no root, but endures only for a while, and when trouble or persecution arises on account of the word, that person immediately falls away. As for what was sown among thorns, this is the one who hears the word, but the cares of the world and the lure of wealth choke the word, and it yields nothing.

"But as for what was sown on good soil, this is the one who hears the word and understands it, who indeed bears fruit and yields, in one case a hundredfold, in another sixty, and in another thirty."

The Gospel of the Lord. **Praise to you, Lord Jesus Christ.**

Saul was a man who bullied and terrorized the first Christians. One day, he saw the risen Jesus and the experience changed his whole life. When he was baptized he changed his name to Paul and became a great apostle, travelling to cities all around the Mediterranean Sea to tell people about the love of Jesus. Several letters he wrote are now in the Bible.

When we speak of God's glory, we are talking about God's power, importance and splendour.

When we are distracted from our friendship with God, our lives are ones of futility or aimlessness. God wants us to direct our lives to following the Spirit.

Parables are brief stories or wise sayings that Jesus used to teach a certain message. Jesus used everyday situations to help his listeners understand what he meant. The parables invite us to change our lives and turn to God.

A sower is a farmer who is planting seeds by hand. In this parable, the seeds represent the word of God. Sometimes it bears fruit and sometimes it does not. We must try to be fertile ground for the word of God.

A plant needs a good root system, deep and strong, in order to survive times of stress. We also need a solid and secure faith, rooted deep in the Spirit of God, dwelling in our hearts.

16th Sunday in Ordinary Time

There is no god besides you, Lord,
whose care is for all people,
to whom you should prove that you have not judged unjustly.

For your strength is the source of righteousness,
and your sovereignty over all causes you to spare all.
For you show your strength
when people doubt the completeness of your power,
and you rebuke any insolence among those who know it.
Although you are sovereign in strength,
you judge with mildness,
and with great forbearance you govern us;
for you have power to act whenever you choose.

Through such works you have taught your people
that the righteous must be kind,
and you have filled your children with good hope,
because you give repentance for sins.

The word of the Lord. **Thanks be to God.**

Psalm 86

R̸ **Lord, you are good and forgiving.**

You, O Lord, are good and forgiving,
abounding in steadfast love to all who call on you.
Give ear, O Lord, to my prayer;
listen to my cry of supplication. R̸

All the nations you have made shall come
and bow down before you, O Lord,
and shall glorify your name.
For you are great and do wondrous things;
you alone are God. R̸

But you, O Lord, are a God merciful and gracious,
slow to anger and abounding in steadfast love
and faithfulness.
Turn to me and be gracious to me.
Give your strength to your servant. R̸

A reading from the Letter of Saint Paul to the Romans (8.26-27)

Brothers and sisters: The Spirit helps us in our weakness; for we do not know how to pray as we ought, but that very Spirit intercedes with sighs too deep for words.

And God, who searches the heart, knows what is the mind of the Spirit, because the Spirit intercedes for the saints according to the will of God.

The word of the Lord. **Thanks be to God.**

A reading from the holy Gospel according to Matthew (13.24-43)

The shorter reading ends at the asterisks.

Jesus put before the crowds a parable: "The kingdom of heaven may be compared to someone who sowed good seed in his field; but while everybody was asleep, an enemy came and sowed weeds among the wheat, and then went away.

"So when the plants came up and bore grain, then the weeds appeared as well. And the slaves of the householder came and said to him, 'Master, did you not sow good seed in your field? Where, then, did these weeds come from?' He answered, 'An enemy has done this.' The slaves said to him, 'Then do you want us to go and gather them?' But he replied, 'No; for in gathering the weeds you would uproot the wheat along with them. Let both of them grow together until the harvest; and at harvest time I will tell the reapers, Collect the weeds first and bind them in bundles to be burned, but gather the wheat into my barn.'"

Jesus put before them another parable: "The kingdom of heaven is like a mustard seed that someone took and sowed in his field; it is the smallest of all the seeds, but when it has grown it is the greatest of shrubs and becomes a tree, so that the birds of the air come and make nests in its branches."

He told them another parable: "The kingdom of heaven is like yeast that a woman took and mixed in with three measures of flour until all of it was leavened."

* * *

Jesus told the crowds all these things in parables; without a parable he told them nothing. This was to fulfill what had been spoken through the Prophet: "I will open my mouth to speak in parables; I will proclaim what has been hidden from the foundation of the world."

Then Jesus left the crowds and went into the house. And his disciples approached him, saying, "Explain to us the parable of the weeds of the field." He answered, "The one who sows the good seed is the Son of Man; the field is the world, and the good seed are the children of the kingdom; the weeds are the children of the evil one, and the enemy who sowed them is the devil; the harvest is the end of the age, and the reapers are Angels.

"Just as the weeds are collected and burned up with fire, so will it be at the end of the age. The Son of Man will send his Angels, and they will collect out of his kingdom all causes of sin and all evildoers, and they will throw them into the furnace of fire, where there will be weeping and gnashing of teeth. Then the righteous will shine like the sun in the kingdom of their Father. Let anyone with ears listen!"

The Gospel of the Lord. **Praise to you, Lord Jesus Christ.**

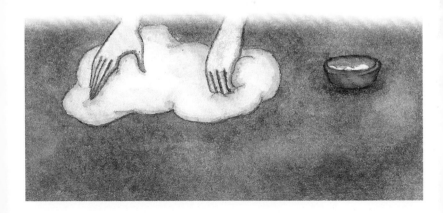

The book of Wisdom was written not long before Jesus was born. It urges us to make good decisions in life. It teaches about justice and fairness.

To spare someone is to decide not to punish them or to relieve them of trouble.

To judge is to decide a question based on the evidence. For example, in court a judge may decide whether someone is innocent or guilty of a crime. God judges with patience and mercy.

To intercede means to ask for something on behalf of another person.

When weeds grow with a crop, they take water and nutrition away from the good plants. A weed-free field will produce a better harvest.

Both the weeds and the wheat are tied into their own bundles, to make them easier to handle for the fieldworkers.

Yeast is added to bread dough to make it rise. As the yeast ferments, gas is produced and the dough expands. The bread is then light and easy to eat.

17th Sunday in Ordinary Time

At Gibeon the Lord appeared to Solomon in a dream by night; and God said, "Ask what I should give you." And Solomon said, "You have shown great and steadfast love to your servant my father David, because he walked before you in faithfulness, in righteousness, and in uprightness of heart toward you; and you have kept for him this great and steadfast love, and have given him a son to sit on his throne today.

"And now, O Lord my God, you have made your servant king in place of my father David, although I am only a little child; I do not know how to go out or come in. And your servant is in the midst of the people whom you have chosen, a great people, so numerous they cannot be numbered or counted. Give your servant therefore an understanding mind to govern your people, able to discern between good and evil; for who can govern this, your great people?"

It pleased the Lord that Solomon had asked this. God said to him, "Because you have asked this, and have not asked for yourself long life or riches, or for the life of your enemies, but have asked for yourself understanding to discern what is right, I now do according to your word. Indeed I give you a wise and discerning mind; no one like you has been before you and no one like you shall arise after you."

The word of the Lord. **Thanks be to God.**

R. **Lord, how I love your law!**

The Lord is my portion;
I promise to keep your words.
The law of your mouth is better to me
than thousands of gold and silver pieces. R.

Let your steadfast love become my comfort
according to your promise to your servant.
Let your mercy come to me, that I may live;
for your law is my delight. R.

Truly I love your commandments more than gold,
more than fine gold.
Truly I direct my steps by all your precepts;
I hate every false way. R.

Your decrees are wonderful;
therefore my soul keeps them.
The unfolding of your words gives light;
it imparts understanding to the simple. R.

A reading from the Letter of Saint Paul to the Romans (8.28-30)

Brothers and sisters: We know that all things work together for good for those who love God, who are called according to his purpose.

For those whom God foreknew he also predestined to be conformed to the image of his Son, in order that he might be the firstborn among many brothers and sisters.

And those whom God predestined he also called; and those whom he called he also justified; and those whom he justified he also glorified.

The word of the Lord. **Thanks be to God.**

The shorter reading ends at the asterisks.

Jesus spoke to the crowds: "The kingdom of heaven is like treasure hidden in a field, which someone found and hid; then in his joy he goes and sells all that he has and buys that field.

"Again, the kingdom of heaven is like a merchant in search of fine pearls; on finding one pearl of great value, he went and sold all that he had and bought it.

"Again, the kingdom of heaven is like a net that was thrown into the sea and caught fish of every kind; when it was full, they drew it ashore, sat down, and put the good into baskets but threw out the bad.

* * *

"So it will be at the end of the age. The Angels will come out and separate the evil from the righteous and throw them into the furnace of fire, where there will be weeping and gnashing of teeth.

"Have you understood all this?" They answered, "Yes." And he said to them, "Therefore every scribe who has been trained for the kingdom of heaven is like the master of a household who brings out of his treasure what is new and what is old."

The Gospel of the Lord. **Praise to you, Lord Jesus Christ.**

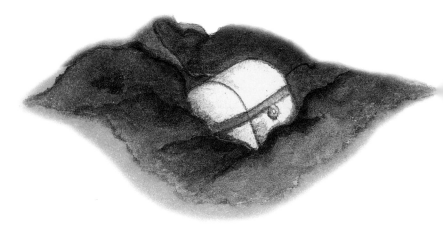

Solomon was the king of Israel after his father, David. He lived 1,000 years before Christ. Solomon was a wise and prudent king.

An understanding mind is one that relies not only on what the eye sees, but also on the wisdom of the heart. Solomon knew God as the Creator of all and made his decisions based on this deep knowledge.

God's purpose from the beginning has been the salvation of all creation. God wants all humankind to be live in friendship with him.

God knows us before we are born, and we are predestined or meant to be God's children. We should live like Jesus did, loving the Father and taking care of others, especially those who are weaker or in need. This is the destiny God has for us.

When we hurt others, we break our friendship with God. But Jesus came to restore our friendship with God, and we are justified or brought back to friendship with God by our faith in Jesus.

By comparing the kingdom of heaven to treasure, Jesus is saying that life with God is more valuable than anything we can find or buy on earth. It is priceless.

18th Sunday in Ordinary Time

Thus says the Lord:
"Everyone who thirsts,
come to the waters;
and you that have no money,
come, buy and eat!
Come, buy wine and milk
without money and without price.

"Why do you spend your money for that which is not bread,
and your labour for that which does not satisfy?
Listen carefully to me, and eat what is good,
and delight yourselves in rich food.

"Incline your ear, and come to me;
listen, so that you may live.
I will make with you an everlasting covenant,
my steadfast, sure love for David."

The word of the Lord. **Thanks be to God.**

Psalm 145

R. **You open your hand to feed us, Lord, and satisfy our needs.**

The Lord is gracious and merciful,
slow to anger and abounding in steadfast love.
The Lord is good to all,
and his compassion is over all that he has made. R.

The eyes of all look to you,
and you give them their food in due season.
You open your hand,
satisfying the desire of every living thing. R.

The Lord is just in all his ways,
and kind in all his doings.
The Lord is near to all who call on him,
to all who call on him in truth. R.

Brothers and sisters: Who will separate us from the love of Christ? Will hardship, or distress, or persecution, or famine, or nakedness, or peril, or sword? No, in all these things we are more than conquerors through him who loved us.

For I am convinced that neither death, nor life, nor Angels, nor rulers, nor things present, nor things to come, nor powers, nor height, nor depth, nor anything else in all creation, will be able to separate us from the love of God in Christ Jesus our Lord.

The word of the Lord. **Thanks be to God.**

When Jesus heard that Herod had beheaded John the Baptist, he withdrew in a boat to a deserted place by himself. But when the crowds heard it, they followed him on foot from the towns. When he went ashore, Jesus saw a great crowd; and he had compassion for them and cured their sick.

When it was evening, the disciples came to him and said, "This is a deserted place, and the hour is now late; send the crowds away so that they may go into the villages and buy food for themselves." Jesus said to them, "They need not go away; you give them something to eat." They replied, "We have nothing here but five loaves and two fish." And he said, "Bring them here to me."

Then Jesus ordered the crowds to sit down on the grass. Taking the five loaves and the two fish, he looked up to heaven, and blessed and broke the loaves, and gave them to the disciples, and the disciples gave them to the crowds.

And all ate and were filled; and they took up what was left over of the broken pieces, twelve baskets full. And those who ate were about five thousand men, besides women and children.

The Gospel of the Lord. **Praise to you, Lord Jesus Christ.**

A covenant is a promise between two people or groups. In the first covenant, also called the Old Testament, God promised to care for his people and the people agreed to worship only God. In the new covenant through Jesus, also called the New Testament, God renews his promise and we agree to love one another and God.

We all know hardship at some time in our lives, times of suffering or misfortune. God's word teaches us that not even these hard times can keep God's love from us. God's love is stronger than anything.

Angels are God's messengers. Because they live close to God, they are powerful. But even angels cannot keep God's love away from God's children, if indeed they wanted to. God's love is stronger even than angels.

John the Baptist was the son of Zechariah and Elizabeth, a cousin of the Virgin Mary. He told people that Jesus was coming soon. He was called John the Baptist because he baptized many people.

Jesus often went to a deserted place by himself. Here, he would pray to his Father. He looked for places where there were no distractions, so that he could pray in silence and listen to God in his heart. This is one of the most important lessons about prayer that Jesus taught us.

19th Sunday in Ordinary Time

When Elijah reached Horeb, the mountain of God, he came to a cave, and spent the night there. Then the word of the Lord came to him, saying, "Go out and stand on the mountain before the Lord, for the Lord is about to pass by."

Now there was a great wind, so strong that it was splitting mountains and breaking rocks in pieces before the Lord, but the Lord was not in the wind; and after the wind an earthquake, but the Lord was not in the earthquake; and after the earthquake a fire, but the Lord was not in the fire; and after the fire a sound of sheer silence.

When Elijah heard it, he wrapped his face in his mantle and went out and stood at the entrance of the cave.

The word of the Lord. **Thanks be to God.**

Psalm 85

R̶ **Show us your steadfast love, O Lord,
and grant us your salvation.**

Let me hear what God the Lord will speak,
for he will speak peace to his people.
Surely his salvation is at hand for those who fear him,
that his glory may dwell in our land. R̶

Steadfast love and faithfulness will meet;
righteousness and peace will kiss each other.
Faithfulness will spring up from the ground,
and righteousness will look down from the sky. R̶

The Lord will give what is good,
and our land will yield its increase.
Righteousness will go before him,
and will make a path for his steps. R̶

Brothers and sisters: I am speaking the truth in Christ. I am not lying; my conscience confirms it by the Holy Spirit. I have great sorrow and unceasing anguish in my heart.

For I could wish that I myself were accursed and cut off from Christ for the sake of my own people, my kindred according to the flesh. They are children of Israel, and to them belong the adoption, the glory, the covenants, the giving of the law, the worship, and the promises; to them belong the patriarchs, and from them, according to the flesh, comes the Christ, who is over all, God be blessed forever. Amen.

The word of the Lord. **Thanks be to God.**

Immediately after feeding the crowd with the five loaves and two fish, Jesus made the disciples get into the boat and go on ahead to the other side, while he dismissed the crowds. And after he had dismissed the crowds, he went up the mountain by himself to pray.

When evening came, he was there alone, but by this time the boat, battered by the waves, was far from the land, for the wind was against them.

And early in the morning Jesus came walking toward them on the sea. But when the disciples saw him walking on the sea, they were terrified, saying, "It is a ghost!" And they cried out in fear. But immediately Jesus spoke to them and said, "Take heart, it is I; do not be afraid."

Peter answered him, "Lord, if it is you, command me to come to you on the water." Jesus said, "Come." So Peter got out of the boat, started walking on the water, and came toward Jesus. But when he noticed the strong wind, he became frightened, and beginning to sink, he cried out, "Lord, save me!"

Jesus immediately reached out his hand and caught him, saying to him, "You of little faith, why did you doubt?" When they got into the boat, the wind ceased. And those in the boat worshipped him, saying, "Truly you are the Son of God."

The Gospel of the Lord. **Praise to you, Lord Jesus Christ.**

The prophet Elijah lived about 900 years before Jesus. He taught the people about God.

Mount Horeb (or Mount Sinai, as it is also called) is a place where God often visited his people. God spoke to Moses there and gave him the Ten Commandments.

The patriarchs were the ancestors of the people of Israel. Abraham, Isaac and Jacob were all known as patriarchs. God promised them that this people would become a great nation.

Amen is a Hebrew word that means 'so be it' or 'I know this is true.' By saying Amen after hearing or saying a prayer, we agree with what it says.

The apostles worshipped Jesus because they recognized that he was more than a man. Jesus is true God and true man. Worship is a gesture that recognizes the greatness of the one being worshipped.

20th Sunday in Ordinary Time

Thus says the Lord: "Maintain justice, and do what is right, for soon my salvation will come, and my deliverance be revealed.

"And the foreigners who join themselves to the Lord, to minister to him, to love the name of the Lord, and to be his servants, all who keep the Sabbath, and do not profane it, and hold fast my covenant—these I will bring to my holy mountain, and make them joyful in my house of prayer; their burnt offerings and their sacrifices will be accepted on my altar; for my house shall be called a house of prayer for all peoples."

The word of the Lord. **Thanks be to God.**

Psalm 67

R. **Let the peoples praise you, O God,
let all the peoples praise you!**

May God be gracious to us and bless us
and make his face to shine upon us,
that your way may be known upon earth,
your saving power among all nations. R.

Let the nations be glad and sing for joy,
for you judge the peoples with equity
and guide the nations upon earth.
Let the peoples praise you, O God;
let all the peoples praise you. R.

The earth has yielded its increase;
God, our God, has blessed us.
May God continue to bless us;
let all the ends of the earth revere him. R.

A reading from the Letter of Saint Paul to the Romans (11.13-15, 29-32)

Brothers and sisters: Now I am speaking to you Gentiles. Inasmuch then as I am an Apostle to the Gentiles, I glorify my ministry in order to make my own flesh and blood jealous, and thus save some of them. For if their rejection is the reconciliation of the world, what will their acceptance be but life from the dead!

The gifts and the calling of God are irrevocable. Just as you were once disobedient to God but have now received mercy because of their disobedience, so they have now been disobedient in order that, by the mercy shown to you, they too may now receive mercy. For God has imprisoned all in disobedience so that he may be merciful to all.

The word of the Lord. **Thanks be to God.**

A reading from the holy Gospel according to Matthew (15.21-28)

Jesus went away to the district of Tyre and Sidon. A Canaanite woman from that region came out, and started shouting, "Have mercy on me, Lord, Son of David; my daughter is tormented by a demon." But he did not answer her at all.

And his disciples came and urged him, saying, "Send her away, for she keeps shouting after us." He answered, "I was sent only to the lost sheep of the house of Israel."

But the woman came and knelt before him, saying, "Lord, help me." He answered, "It is not fair to take the children's food and throw it to the dogs." She said, "Yes, Lord, yet even the dogs eat the crumbs that fall from their masters' table."

Then Jesus answered her, "Woman, great is your faith! Let it be done for you as you wish." And her daughter was healed instantly.

The Gospel of the Lord. **Praise to you, Lord Jesus Christ.**

224

Our faith in God requires us to maintain justice—to take care of the rights of others. Working for the dignity and freedom of others is one way of obeying God's commandments.

The Sabbath is the day of the week when human beings rest like God did on the seventh day of creation. It is a chance for us to spend time praising God and enjoying creation. One of the Ten Commandments instructs us to keep the Sabbath holy.

Burnt offerings are a type of sacrifice to God where an animal (such as a dead lamb or calf) is put on a fire. Another type of offering is a libation, a drink-offering that is poured out.

Paul calls himself an Apostle to the Gentiles, meaning a messenger to people who were not Jewish. He wants all people, Jews and Gentiles, to be saved from death by faith in Jesus.

Canaanites were from Canaan. After 40 years in the desert, Moses brought God's people to the land of Canaan, the promised land. In the time of Jesus, people from Canaan were considered foreigners.

House of Israel is one of the many names for the Israelites. Other names include House of David and House of Judah.

When Jesus says, "great is your faith," he is pointing to the confidence the Canaanite woman has. She brings her daughter's illness and her own pain to Jesus, believing that he will help them, even though she is a stranger in their society.

21st Sunday in Ordinary Time

Thus says the Lord God of hosts: Go to the steward, to Shebna, who is master of the household, and say to him:

"I will thrust you from your office, and you will be pulled down from your post. On that day I will call my servant Eliakim son of Hilkiah, and will clothe him with your robe and bind your sash on him. I will commit your authority to his hand, and he shall be a father to the inhabitants of Jerusalem and to the house of Judah.

"I will place on his shoulder the key of the house of David; he shall open, and no one shall shut; he shall shut, and no one shall open. I will fasten him like a peg in a secure place, and he will become a throne of honour to the house of his ancestors."

The word of the Lord. **Thanks be to God.**

Psalm 138

R. **Your steadfast love, O Lord, endures forever.**
Do not forsake the work of your hands.

I give you thanks, O Lord, with my whole heart;
before the Angels I sing your praise;
I bow down toward your holy temple,
    and give thanks to your name
for your steadfast love and your faithfulness. R.

For you have exalted your name
and your word above everything.
On the day I called, you answered me,
you increased my strength of soul. R.

For though the Lord is high, he regards the lowly;
but the haughty he perceives from far away.
Your steadfast love, O Lord, endures forever.
Do not forsake the work of your hands. R.

O the depth of the riches and wisdom and knowledge of God! How unsearchable are his judgments and how inscrutable his ways! "For who has known the mind of the Lord? Or who has been his counsellor?" "Or who has given a gift to him, to receive a gift in return?" For from him and through him and to him are all things. To him be the glory forever. Amen.

The word of the Lord. **Thanks be to God.**

When Jesus came into the district of Caesarea Philippi, he asked his disciples, "Who do people say that the Son of Man is?" And they said, "Some say John the Baptist, but others Elijah, and still others Jeremiah or one of the Prophets."

He said to them, "But who do you say that I am?" Simon Peter answered, "You are the Christ, the Son of the living God."

And Jesus answered him, "Blessed are you, Simon son of Jonah! For flesh and blood has not revealed this to you, but my Father in heaven. And I tell you, you are Peter, and on this rock I will build my Church, and the gates of Hades will not prevail against it. I will give you the keys of the kingdom of heaven, and whatever you bind on earth will be bound in heaven, and whatever you loose on earth will be loosed in heaven."

Then Jesus sternly ordered the disciples not to tell anyone that he was the Christ.

The Gospel of the Lord. **Praise to you, Lord Jesus Christ.**

Shebna's error was to construct a luxurious tomb at a time when many people were in great need. He should have used his wealth in a just way to take care of the needs of others.

House of Judah is one of the many names for the Israelites. Other names include House of David and House of Israel.

When Jesus began to preach, he called himself the Son of Man. This is another way of telling us that he was sent by God.

The Greek word for 'anointed' is Christ. The chosen person was anointed or blessed with holy oil and given a special mission. The Aramaic word meaning 'anointed' is Messiah (Jesus and his disciples spoke Aramaic).

When Simon shows both his understanding and faith in Jesus as the Messiah, Jesus gives him a new name—Peter (from the Greek word *petra* for rock or stone). In many other languages, the name Peter is also related to rock or stone (such as *pierre* in French). Jesus is saying that Peter's faith will be the foundation for the Church's future.

Keys are a symbol of power. Whoever has the keys can enter and leave at will; they can also allow or deny entry. Jesus used this symbol to show that Peter is the person with this power in the early Church.

When Jesus promised Peter, "Whatever you bind on earth will be bound in heaven," he was letting Peter know that Jesus would be with him always, guiding his thoughts and actions through the presence of the Holy Spirit.

22nd Sunday in Ordinary Time

O Lord, you have enticed me, and I was enticed; you have overpowered me, and you have prevailed. I have become a laughingstock all day long; everyone mocks me. For whenever I speak, I must cry out, I must shout, "Violence and destruction!" For the word of the Lord has become for me a reproach and derision all day long.

If I say, "I will not mention him, or speak any more in his name," then within me there is something like a burning fire shut up in my bones; I am weary with holding it in, and I cannot.

The word of the Lord. **Thanks be to God.**

Psalm 63

℟. **My soul thirsts for you, O Lord my God.**

O God, you are my God, I seek you,
my soul thirsts for you;
my flesh faints for you,
as in a dry and weary land where there is no water. ℟.

So I have looked upon you in the sanctuary,
beholding your power and glory.
Because your steadfast love is better than life,
my lips will praise you. ℟.

So I will bless you as long as I live;
I will lift up my hands and call on your name.
My soul is satisfied as with a rich feast,
and my mouth praises you with joyful lips. ℟.

For you have been my help,
and in the shadow of your wings I sing for joy.
My soul clings to you;
your right hand upholds me. ℟.

A reading from the Letter of Saint Paul to the Romans (12.1-2)

I appeal to you, brothers and sisters, by the mercies of God, to present your bodies as a living sacrifice, holy and acceptable to God, which is your spiritual worship. Do not be conformed to this world, but be transformed by the renewing of your minds, so that you may discern what is the will of God—what is good and acceptable and perfect.

The word of the Lord. **Thanks be to God.**

A reading from the holy Gospel according to Matthew (16.21-27)

Jesus began to show his disciples that he must go to Jerusalem and undergo great suffering at the hands of the elders and chief priests and scribes, and be killed, and on the third day be raised.

And Peter took Jesus aside and began to rebuke him, saying, "God forbid it, Lord! This must never happen to you." But he turned and said to Peter, "Get behind me, Satan! You are a stumbling block to me; for you are thinking not as God does, but as humans do."

Then Jesus told his disciples, "If anyone wants to become my follower, let him deny himself and take up his cross and follow me. For whoever wants to save their life will lose it, and whoever loses their life for my sake will find it. For what will it profit anyone to gain the whole world but forfeit their life? Or what will anyone give in return for their life?

"For the Son of Man is to come with his Angels in the glory of his Father, and then he will repay each according to their work."

The Gospel of the Lord. **Praise to you, Lord Jesus Christ.**

Jeremiah lived about 600 years before Jesus. When Jeremiah was still a young boy, God called him to guide the people of Israel back to God. Many people ignored Jeremiah at first and sent him away. But when they faced serious problems and feared that God had stopped loving them, Jeremiah gave them hope that God would not abandon them.

Jeremiah found being a prophet very hard work and he wanted to give it up. But he found he couldn't because the voice of God within him was like an intense fire.

Paul reminds us that God does not want elaborate or expensive sacrifices when we worship. God wants us to offer ourselves and our lives. Paul calls this our spiritual worship.

Satan is one of the names given to the enemy of God and our strongest enemy. Satan works against God and tries to lead people away from God's love. Other names for Satan are the Evil One, Lucifer or the Devil.

To take up our cross means to accept all that comes with being alive, the good and the bad alike, because we are called to follow the path taken by Jesus.

23rd Sunday in Ordinary Time

GENINA

Thus says the Lord: "So you, O son of man, I have made a watchman for the house of Israel; whenever you hear a word from my mouth, you shall give them warning from me.

"If I say to the wicked, 'O wicked one, you shall surely die,' and you do not speak to warn the wicked to turn from their ways, the wicked person shall die in their iniquity, but their blood I will require at your hand.

"But if you warn the wicked person to turn from their ways, and they do not turn from their ways, they shall die in their iniquity, but you will have saved your life."

The word of the Lord. **Thanks be to God.**

Psalm 95

R̰ **O that today you would listen to the voice of the Lord. Do not harden your hearts!**

O come, let us sing to the Lord;
let us make a joyful noise to the rock of our salvation!
Let us come into his presence with thanksgiving;
let us make a joyful noise to him with songs of praise! R̰

O come, let us worship and bow down,
let us kneel before the Lord, our Maker!
For he is our God, and we are the people of his pasture,
and the sheep of his hand. R̰

O that today you would listen to his voice!
Do not harden your hearts, as at Meribah,
as on the day at Massah in the wilderness,
when your ancestors tested me,
and put me to the proof,
though they had seen my work. R̰

A reading from the Letter of Saint Paul to the Romans (13.8-10)

Brothers and sisters: Owe no one anything, except to love one another; for the one who loves another has fulfilled the law.

The commandments, "You shall not commit adultery; You shall not murder; You shall not steal; You shall not covet"; and any other commandment, are summed up in this word, "Love your neighbour as yourself."

Love does no wrong to a neighbour; therefore, love is the fulfilling of the law.

The word of the Lord. **Thanks be to God.**

A reading from the holy Gospel according to Matthew (18.15-20)

Jesus spoke to his disciples. "If your brother or sister sins against you, go and point out the fault when the two of you are alone. If he or she listens to you, you have regained your brother or sister. But if the person does not listen, take one or two others along with you, so that every word may be confirmed by the evidence of two or three witnesses. If the person refuses to listen to them, tell it to the Church; and if that person refuses to listen even to the Church, let such a one be to you as a Gentile and a tax collector.

"Truly I tell you, whatever you bind on earth will be bound in heaven, and whatever you loose on earth will be loosed in heaven. Again, truly I tell you, if two of you agree on earth about anything you ask, it will be done for you by my Father in heaven. For where two or three are gathered in my name, I am there among them."

The Gospel of the Lord. **Praise to you, Lord Jesus Christ.**

Ezekiel was one of the most important prophets in Israel. He lived during a time when many of the people of Jerusalem were taken prisoner and forced to live in another place, Babylon. The king and Ezekiel were taken away, too. Ezekiel helped the people follow God's ways even though they were far from home.

Ezekiel was the watchman or sentinel for Israel because it was his mission to teach the people how to live as God wants and to warn them away from error and danger.

Love one another—these words sum up what every Christian must do. All the commandments and all that Jesus said and did have their foundation in this simple phrase.

Jesus tells us to point out to our friends anything we see that we feel is wrong. But Jesus tells us also to do this with love in our hearts, with respect for the other person.

Gentiles are people who are not Jewish. At the time of Jesus, Gentiles could not participate fully in Jewish society because they were excluded from temple life.

The Jews didn't like tax collectors because they worked for the Romans who were enemies of Israel. Also, many tax collectors cheated people and took more money than they needed for taxes.

Jesus shows us that God listens to our prayers. It is especially important to pray—"where two or three are gathered in my name" —with all people who believe in God.

24th Sunday in Ordinary Time

Anger and wrath, these are abominations, yet a sinner holds on to them. The vengeful person will face the Lord's vengeance, for he keeps a strict account of their sins. Forgive your neighbour the wrong that is done, and then your sins will be pardoned when you pray.

Does anyone harbour anger against another, and expect healing from the Lord? If one has no mercy toward another like oneself, can one then seek pardon for one's own sins? If one who is but flesh harbours wrath, who will make an atoning sacrifice for that person's sins?

Remember the end of your life, and set enmity aside; remember corruption and death, and be true to the commandments. Remember the commandments, and do not be angry with your neighbour; remember the covenant of the Most High, and overlook faults.

The word of the Lord. **Thanks be to God.**

Psalm 103

R. **The Lord is merciful and gracious;
slow to anger, and abounding in steadfast love.**

Bless the Lord, O my soul,
and all that is within me, bless his holy name.
Bless the Lord, O my soul,
and do not forget all his benefits. R.

It is the Lord who forgives all your iniquity,
who heals all your diseases,
who redeems your life from the Pit,
who crowns you with steadfast love and mercy. R.

He will not always accuse,
nor will he keep his anger forever.
He does not deal with us according to our sins,
nor repay us according to our iniquities. R.

For as the heavens are high above the earth,
so great is his steadfast love toward those who fear him;
as far as the east is from the west,
so far he removes our transgressions from us. R.

Brothers and sisters: We do not live to ourselves, and we do not die to ourselves. If we live, we live to the Lord, and if we die, we die to the Lord; so then, whether we live or whether we die, we are the Lord's. For to this end Christ died and lived again, so that he might be Lord of both the dead and the living.

The word of the Lord. **Thanks be to God.**

Peter came and said to Jesus, "Lord, how often should I forgive my brother or sister if they sin against me? As many as seven times?" Jesus said to him, "Not seven times, but, I tell you, seventy-seven times.

"For this reason the kingdom of heaven may be compared to a king who wished to settle accounts with his slaves. When he began the reckoning, one who owed him ten thousand talents was brought to him; and, as he could not pay, his lord ordered him to be sold, together with his wife and children and all his possessions, and payment to be made. So the slave fell on his knees before him, saying, 'Have patience with me, and I will pay you everything.' The lord of that slave released him and forgave him the debt.

"But that same slave, as he went out, came upon one of his fellow slaves who owed him a hundred denarii; and seizing him by the throat, he said, 'Pay what you owe.' Then his fellow slave fell down and pleaded with him, 'Have patience with me, and I will pay you.' But he refused; then he went and threw him into prison until he would pay the debt.

"When his fellow slaves saw what had happened, they were greatly distressed, and they went and reported to their lord all that had taken place. Then his lord summoned him and said to him, 'You wicked slave! I forgave you all that debt because you pleaded with me. Should you not have had mercy on your fellow slave, as I had mercy on you?' And in anger his lord handed him over to be tortured until he would pay his entire debt.

"So my heavenly Father will also do to every one of you, if you do not forgive your brother or sister from your heart."

The Gospel of the Lord. **Praise to you, Lord Jesus Christ.**

Abominations are hateful things, things that even make us feel sick. In this reading, Sirach is reminding us that when we hold onto our anger and wish evil on another person, we are offending God in the strongest possible way.

This verse in the reading, telling us to **forgive** our neighbour, sounds just like part of the Our Father: Forgive us our trespasses, as we forgive those who trespass against us. From the very beginning, God has called his people to be a forgiving people.

Iniquities and **transgressions** are other words for sins or trespasses—things we do to other people that are wrong, unjust or unkind.

The number **seven** indicates something complete, like seven days in a week—so Peter is suggesting that forgiving seven times would be enough. But Jesus replies with **seventy-seven**—a super-seven—to show that we must never stop forgiving others.

Jesus uses sums of money in this parable to show how extravagant God is in his mercy, and how stingy we can be in ours. **Ten thousand talents** is a huge debt—one that no person could ever hope to repay. A **hundred denarii** is a much smaller amount—a denarius represented a day's pay for a labourer.

25th Sunday in Ordinary Time

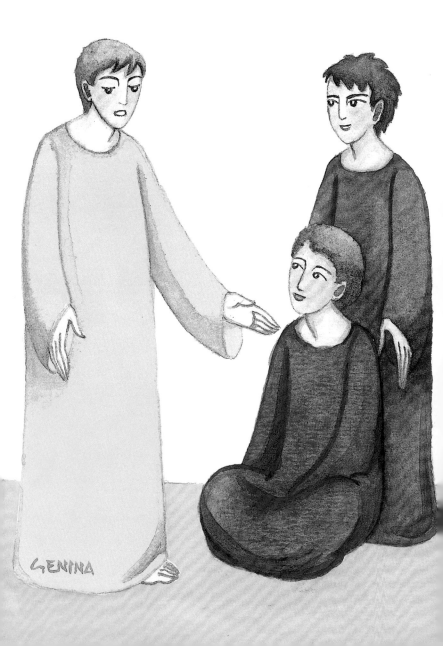

Seek the Lord while he may be found,
call upon him while he is near;
let the wicked person forsake their way,
and the unrighteous person their thoughts;
let that person return to the Lord that he may have mercy on them,
and to our God, for he will abundantly pardon.

For my thoughts are not your thoughts,
nor are your ways my ways, says the Lord.
For as the heavens are higher than the earth,
so are my ways higher than your ways
and my thoughts than your thoughts.

The word of the Lord. **Thanks be to God.**

Psalm 145

R. **The Lord is near to all who call on him.**

Every day I will bless you,
and praise your name forever and ever.
Great is the Lord, and greatly to be praised;
his greatness is unsearchable. R.

The Lord is gracious and merciful,
slow to anger and abounding in steadfast love.
The Lord is good to all,
and his compassion is over all that he has made. R.

The Lord is just in all his ways,
and kind in all his doings.
The Lord is near to all who call on him,
to all who call on him in truth. R.

Brothers and sisters: Christ will be exalted now as always in my body, whether by life or by death. For to me, living is Christ and dying is gain. If I am to live in the flesh, that means fruitful labour for me; and I do not know which I prefer. I am hard pressed between the two: my desire is to depart and be with Christ, for that is far better; but to remain in the flesh is more necessary for you. Live your life in a manner worthy of the Gospel of Christ.

The word of the Lord. **Thanks be to God.**

Jesus spoke this parable to his disciples. "The kingdom of heaven is like a landowner who went out early in the morning to hire labourers for his vineyard. After agreeing with the labourers for the usual daily wage, he sent them into his vineyard. When he went out about nine o'clock, he saw others standing idle in the marketplace; and he said to them, 'You also go into the vineyard, and I will pay you whatever is right.' So they went.

"When he went out again about noon and about three o'clock, he did the same. And about five o'clock he went out and found others standing around; and he said to them, 'Why are you standing here idle all day?' They said to him, 'Because no one has hired us.' He said to them, 'You also go into the vineyard.'

"When evening came, the owner of the vineyard said to his manager, 'Call the labourers and give them their pay, beginning with the last and then going to the first.' When those hired about five o'clock came, each of them received the usual daily wage.

"Now when the first came, they thought they would receive more; but each of them also received the usual daily wage. And when they received it, they grumbled against the landowner, saying, 'These last worked only one hour, and you have made them equal to us who have borne the burden of the day and the scorching heat.' But he replied to one of them, 'Friend, I am doing you no wrong; did you not agree with me for the usual daily wage? Take what belongs to you and go; I choose to give to this last the same as I give to you. Am I not allowed to do what I choose with what belongs to me? Or are you envious because I am generous?'

"So the last will be first, and the first will be last."

The Gospel of the Lord. **Praise to you, Lord Jesus Christ.**

To forsake means to abandon or give up something. Isaiah was telling the people of Israel that they had fallen away from God and needed to journey back to the Lord their God.

God's thoughts are wise and loving, full of compassion and mercy. We can trust in God, even though we cannot understand the greatness of God.

When he was in prison Paul wrote to the Philippians, a community of Christians in Philippi in Greece. He thanked them for their help and encouraged them to keep their faith in Jesus strong.

Paul reminds us that when we hear the word of God and act on it, Jesus is exalted or praised through our actions.

In the kingdom of heaven, all people will be brought together in Jesus. We will all live like brothers and sisters, sharing in God's abundant love and mercy.

A vineyard is a farm where grapevines are grown. At the time of Jesus, there were many vineyards in Israel. Grapes are an important crop because wine is made from the grapes.

26th Sunday in Ordinary Time

GENINA

Thus says the Lord: "You object, O House of Israel! You say, 'The way of the Lord is unfair.' Hear now, O house of Israel: Is my way unfair? Is it not your ways that are unfair?

"When the righteous person turns away from their righteousness and commits iniquity, they shall die for it; for the iniquity that they have committed they shall die.

"Again, when the wicked person turns away from the wickedness they have committed and does what is lawful and right, they shall save their life. Because that person considered and turned away from all the transgressions that they had committed, they shall surely live; they shall not die."

The word of the Lord. **Thanks be to God.**

Psalm 25

R. **Lord, be mindful of your mercy.**

Make me to know your ways, O Lord;
teach me your paths.
Lead me in your truth, and teach me,
for you are the God of my salvation. R.

Be mindful of your mercy, O Lord,
and of your steadfast love,
for they have been from of old.
According to your steadfast love remember me,
for the sake of your goodness, O Lord! R.

Good and upright is the Lord;
therefore he instructs sinners in the way.
He leads the humble in what is right,
and teaches the humble his way. R.

The shorter version ends at the asterisks.

Brothers and sisters: If there is any encouragement in Christ, any consolation from love, any sharing in the Spirit, any compassion and sympathy, then make my joy complete: be of the same mind, having the same love, being in full accord and of one mind. Do nothing from selfish ambition or conceit, but in humility regard others as better than yourselves. Let each of you look not to your own interests, but to the interests of others.

Let the same mind be in you that was in Christ Jesus.

* * *

who, though he was in the form of God,
did not regard equality with God as something to be exploited,
but emptied himself, taking the form of a slave,
being born in human likeness.
And being found in human form,
he humbled himself
and became obedient to the point of death—
even death on a cross.

Therefore God highly exalted him
and gave him the name that is above every name,
so that at the name of Jesus every knee should bend,
in heaven and on earth and under the earth,
and every tongue should confess that Jesus Christ is Lord,
to the glory of God the Father.

The word of the Lord. **Thanks be to God.**

Jesus said to the chief priests and the elders of the people: "What do you think? A man had two sons; he went to the first and said, 'Son, go and work in the vineyard today.' He answered, 'I will not'; but later he changed his mind and went. The father went to the second and said the same; and he answered, 'I am going, sir'; but he did not go. Which of the two did the will of his father?" They said, "The first."

Jesus said to them, "Truly I tell you, the tax collectors and the prostitutes are going into the kingdom of God ahead of you. For John came to you in the way of righteousness and you did not believe him, but the tax collectors and the prostitutes believed him; and even after you saw it, you did not change your minds and believe him."

The Gospel of the Lord. **Praise to you, Lord Jesus Christ.**

In the Old Testament, to be righteous means to follow the laws Moses gave to the people of Israel.

When we follow God's commandments, we show that we have considered or thought deeply about our way of life and are determined to live as children of God.

Humility means knowing we are children of God without feeling too important. We accept all the qualities God gave us—the ones we think are not so good as well as our talents.

When the son in the parable changed his mind, he regretted his earlier decision. He wanted to be an obedient child and show by his actions that he loved his father. In our lives, our actions should show that we are followers of Jesus.

27th Sunday in Ordinary Time

Let me sing for my beloved my love song concerning his vineyard:

"My beloved had a vineyard on a very fertile hill. He dug it and cleared it of stones, and planted it with choice vines; he built a watchtower in the midst of it, and hewed out a wine vat in it; he expected it to yield grapes, but it yielded wild grapes.

"And now, inhabitants of Jerusalem and people of Judah, judge between me and my vineyard. What more was there to do for my vineyard that I have not done in it? When I expected it to yield grapes, why did it yield wild grapes?

"And now I will tell you what I will do to my vineyard. I will remove its hedge, and it shall be devoured; I will break down its wall, and it shall be trampled down. I will make it a waste; it shall not be pruned or hoed, and it shall be overgrown with briers and thorns; I will also command the clouds that they rain no rain upon it. For the vineyard of the Lord of hosts is the house of Israel, and the people of Judah are his pleasant planting; he expected justice, but saw bloodshed; righteousness, but heard a cry!"

The word of the Lord. **Thanks be to God.**

R̶ **The vineyard of the Lord is the house of Israel.**

You brought a vine out of Egypt;
you drove out the nations and planted it.
It sent out its branches to the sea,
and its shoots to the River. R̶

Why then have you broken down its walls,
so that all who pass along the way pluck its fruit?
The boar from the forest ravages it,
and all that move in the field feed on it. R̶

Turn again, O God of hosts;
look down from heaven, and see;
have regard for this vine,
the stock that your right hand planted. R̶

Then we will never turn back from you;
give us life, and we will call on your name.
Restore us, O Lord God of hosts;
let your face shine, that we may be saved. R̶

A reading from the Letter of Saint Paul to the Philippians (4.6-9)

Brothers and sisters: Do not worry about anything, but in everything by prayer and supplication with thanksgiving let your requests be made known to God. And the peace of God, which surpasses all understanding, will guard your hearts and your minds in Christ Jesus.

Finally, brothers and sisters, whatever is true, whatever is honourable, whatever is just, whatever is pure, whatever is pleasing, whatever is commendable, if there is any excellence and if there is anything worthy of praise, think about these things. Keep on doing the things that you have learned and received and heard and seen in me, and the God of peace will be with you.

The word of the Lord. **Thanks be to God.**

Jesus said to the chief priests and the elders of the people: "Listen to another parable. There was a landowner who planted a vineyard, put a fence around it, dug a wine press in it, and built a watchtower. Then he leased it to tenants and went to another country.

"When the harvest time had come, he sent his slaves to the tenants to collect his produce. But the tenants seized his slaves and beat one, killed another, and stoned another. Again he sent other slaves, more than the first; and they treated them in the same way.

"Finally he sent his son to them, saying, 'They will respect my son.' But when the tenants saw the son, they said to themselves, 'This is the heir; come, let us kill him and get his inheritance.' So they seized him, threw him out of the vineyard, and killed him.

"Now when the owner of the vineyard comes, what will he do to those tenants?" They said to him, "He will put those wretches to a miserable death, and lease the vineyard to other tenants who will give him the produce at the harvest time."

Jesus said to them, "Have you never read in the Scriptures:

'The stone that the builders rejected
has become the cornerstone;
this was the Lord's doing,
and it is amazing in our eyes'?

"Therefore I tell you, the kingdom of God will be taken away from you and given to a people that produces the fruits of the kingdom."

The Gospel of the Lord. **Praise to you, Lord Jesus Christ.**

My beloved is another way of saying 'the person I love.' Israel is God's vineyard and God cares for his vineyard with great love and attention.

A waste is a dry, lifeless place where nothing grows.

Briers are wild thorny plants that grow in untended fields.

Justice promotes peace. But injustice brings about bloodshed and destruction. We must work for justice in our world.

God of peace is a name for God. When we follow what God teaches, peace becomes possible—not only peace between enemies, but peace in our hearts too.

Elders are older people who have a great deal of life experience and wisdom. They help us make wise choices.

A wine press is used to squeeze the juice from grapes, so that wine can be made from the juice. Presses are also used to make cider from apples and olive oil from olives.

28th Sunday in Ordinary Time

On this mountain the Lord of hosts will make for all peoples a feast of rich food, a feast of well-aged wines, of rich food filled with marrow, of well-aged wines strained clear.

And he will destroy on this mountain the shroud that is cast over all peoples, the sheet that is spread over all nations; he will swallow up death forever. Then the Lord God will wipe away the tears from all faces, and the disgrace of his people he will take away from all the earth, for the Lord has spoken.

It will be said on that day, "Lo, this is our God; we have waited for him, so that he might save us. This is the Lord for whom we have waited; let us be glad and rejoice in his salvation. For the hand of the Lord will rest on this mountain."

The word of the Lord. **Thanks be to God.**

Psalm 23

R̰. **I shall dwell in the house of the Lord my whole life long.**

The Lord is my shepherd, I shall not want.
He makes me lie down in green pastures;
he leads me beside still waters;
he restores my soul. R̰.

He leads me in right paths for his name's sake.
Even though I walk through the darkest valley, I fear no evil;
for you are with me;
your rod and your staff—they comfort me. R̰.

You prepare a table before me
in the presence of my enemies;
you anoint my head with oil;
my cup overflows. R̰.

Surely goodness and mercy shall follow me
all the days of my life,
and I shall dwell in the house of the Lord
my whole life long. R̰.

Brothers and sisters: I know what it is to have little, and I know what it is to have plenty. In any and all circumstances I have learned the secret of being well-fed and of going hungry, of having plenty and of being in need. I can do all things through him who strengthens me. In any case, it was kind of you to share my distress.

My God will fully satisfy every need of yours according to his riches in glory in Christ Jesus. To our God and Father be glory forever and ever. Amen.

The word of the Lord. **Thanks be to God.**

The shorter version ends at the asterisks.

Once more Jesus spoke to the chief priests and Pharisees in parables: "The kingdom of heaven may be compared to a king who gave a wedding banquet for his son. He sent his slaves to call those who had been invited to the wedding banquet, but they would not come.

"Again he sent other slaves, saying, 'Tell those who have been invited: "Look, I have prepared my dinner, my oxen and my fat calves have been slaughtered, and everything is ready; come to the wedding banquet."' But they made light of it and went away, one to his farm, another to his business, while the rest seized his slaves, mistreated them, and killed them. The king was enraged. He sent his troops, destroyed those murderers, and burned their city.

"Then he said to his slaves, 'The wedding is ready, but those invited were not worthy. Go therefore into the main streets, and invite everyone you find to the wedding banquet.' Those slaves went out into the streets and gathered all whom they found, both good and bad; so the wedding hall was filled with guests.

* * *

"But when the king came in to see the guests, he noticed a man there who was not wearing a wedding robe, and he said to him, 'Friend, how did you get in here without a wedding robe?' And he was speechless. Then the king said to the attendants, 'Bind him hand and foot, and throw him into the outer darkness, where there will be weeping and gnashing of teeth.' For many are called, but few are chosen."

The Gospel of the Lord. **Praise to you, Lord Jesus Christ.**

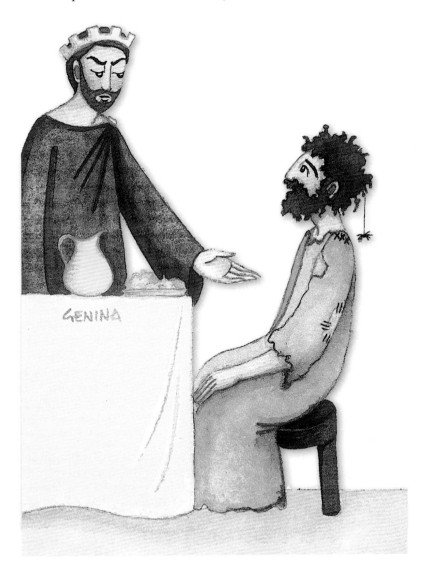

In the Bible, the people of God often encounter God up a mountain. The mountain is a place that is close to God. Jesus also went up the mountain to meet God, such as when he was transfigured.

A feast or banquet with delicious foods and fine wines represents the joyful celebration that God prepares for us. The eucharist gives us a taste of this final celebration.

Amen is a Hebrew word that means 'so be it' or 'I know this is true.' By saying Amen after hearing or saying a prayer, we agree with what it says.

Parables are brief stories or wise sayings that Jesus used to teach a certain message. Jesus used everyday situations to help his listeners understand what he meant. The parables invite us to change our lives and turn to God.

Jesus came to tell us about the kingdom of heaven where people will live peacefully, respecting others and recognizing God as the source of all our joys.

When we are guests at a celebration, we wear our best clothes and often bring a gift. We show that the host and the occasion are important to us. It is the same when we come to Sunday Mass. We come prepared to celebrate, to be attentive, and to share our gifts with God and the community.

29th Sunday in Ordinary Time

Thus says the Lord to his anointed, to Cyrus, whose right hand I have grasped to subdue nations before him and strip kings of their robes, to open doors before him—and the gates shall not be closed:

"For the sake of my servant Jacob, and Israel my chosen, I call you by your name, I surname you, though you do not know me. I am the Lord, and there is no other; besides me there is no god. I arm you, though you do not know me, so that all may know, from the rising of the sun and from the west, that there is no one besides me; I am the Lord, and there is no other."

The word of the Lord. **Thanks be to God.**

Psalm 96

R. **Ascribe to the Lord glory and strength.**

O sing to the Lord a new song;
sing to the Lord, all the earth.
Declare his glory among the nations,
his marvellous works among all the peoples. R.

For great is the Lord, and greatly to be praised;
he is to be revered above all gods.
For all the gods of the peoples are idols,
but the Lord made the heavens. R.

Ascribe to the Lord, O families of the peoples,
ascribe to the Lord glory and strength.
Ascribe to the Lord the glory due his name;
bring an offering, and come into his courts. R.

Worship the Lord in holy splendour;
tremble before him, all the earth.
Say among the nations, "The Lord is king!
He will judge the peoples with equity." R.

From Paul, Silvanus, and Timothy, to the Church of the Thessalonians in God the Father and the Lord Jesus Christ: Grace to you and peace.

We always give thanks to God for all of you and mention you in our prayers, constantly remembering before our God and Father your work of faith and labour of love and steadfastness of hope in our Lord Jesus Christ. For we know, brothers and sisters beloved by God, that he has chosen you, because our message of the Gospel came to you not in word only, but also in power and in the Holy Spirit and with full conviction.

The word of the Lord. **Thanks be to God.**

The Pharisees went and plotted to entrap Jesus in what he said. So they sent their disciples to him, along with the Herodians, saying, "Teacher, we know that you are sincere, and teach the way of God in accordance with truth, and show deference to no one; for you do not regard people with partiality. Tell us, then, what you think. Is it lawful to pay taxes to the emperor, or not?"

But Jesus, aware of their malice, said, "Why are you putting me to the test, you hypocrites? Show me the coin used for the tax." And they brought him a denarius.

Then he said to them, "Whose head is this, and whose title?" They answered, "Caesar's." Then he said to them, "Give therefore to Caesar the things that are Caesar's, and to God the things that are God's."

The Gospel of the Lord. **Praise to you, Lord Jesus Christ.**

To anoint means to 'bless with oil.' In the Bible it can also mean to give someone a mission, an important job. Christians are anointed at baptism and confirmation: our mission is to live as Jesus taught us.

At the time of Isaiah, neighbouring peoples worshipped different gods. But the Lord told Israel that God wasn't just better than the other gods—God is the only God, and there is no other at all.

To judge with equity is to be fair to everyone. The psalmist praises God for his fairness to all people on earth.

Paul wrote two letters to the Thessalonians, Christians who lived in Thessalonica, in Greece. In this letter Paul praises them and encourages them to continue to love one another.

Hypocrites are people who say one thing but do another. They may say they love God, but they don't act in a loving way. Such behaviour demeans the person, hurts others and insults God.

A denarius was a coin worth one day's pay. It had the profile of the Roman emperor stamped on one side of it.

30th Sunday in Ordinary Time

Thus says the Lord: "You shall not wrong or oppress a resident alien, for you were aliens in the land of Egypt. You shall not abuse any widow or orphan. If you do abuse them, when they cry out to me, I will surely heed their cry; my wrath will burn, and I will kill you with the sword, and your wives shall become widows and your children orphans.

"If you lend money to my people, to the poor one among you, you shall not deal with them as a creditor; you shall not exact interest from them. If you take your neighbour's cloak in pawn, you shall restore it to that person before the sun goes down; for it may be their only clothing to use as cover; in what else shall that person sleep? And if that person cries out to me, I will listen, for I am compassionate."

The word of the Lord. **Thanks be to God.**

Psalm 18

R̥ **I love you, O Lord, my strength.**

I love you, O Lord, my strength.
The Lord is my rock, my fortress, and my deliverer.
My God, my rock in whom I take refuge,
my shield, and the source of my salvation, my stronghold. R̥

I call upon the Lord, who is worthy to be praised,
so I shall be saved from my enemies.
From his temple he heard my voice,
and my cry to him reached his ears. R̥

The Lord lives! Blessed be my rock,
and exalted be the God of my salvation.
Great triumphs he gives to his king,
and shows steadfast love to his anointed. R̥

A reading from the first Letter of Saint Paul to the Thessalonians (1.5-10)

Brothers and sisters: You know what kind of persons we proved to be among you for your sake. And you became imitators of us and of the Lord, for in spite of persecution you received the word with joy inspired by the Holy Spirit, so that you became an example to all the believers in Macedonia and in Achaia. For the word of the Lord has sounded forth from you not only in Macedonia and Achaia, but in every place your faith in God has become known, so that we have no need to speak about it. For the people of those regions report about us what kind of welcome we had among you, and how you turned to God from idols, to serve a living and true God, and to wait for his Son from heaven, whom he raised from the dead—Jesus, who rescues us from the wrath that is coming.

The word of the Lord. **Thanks be to God.**

A reading from the holy Gospel according to Matthew (22.34-40)

When the Pharisees heard that Jesus had silenced the Sadducees, they gathered together, and one of them, a lawyer, asked him a question to test him. "Teacher, which commandment in the Law is the greatest?"

Jesus said to him, "'You shall love the Lord your God with all your heart, and with all your soul, and with all your mind.' This is the greatest and first commandment.

"And a second is like it: 'You shall love your neighbour as yourself.' On these two commandments hang all the Law and the Prophets."

The Gospel of the Lord.
Praise to you, Lord Jesus Christ.

268

To oppress or abuse someone is to take advantage of their work in order to benefit oneself. The workers are poorly paid and cannot provide the necessities of life for their families, while the oppressor grows richer and stronger as a result.

A creditor is someone who lends money and charges interest on the loan. Repaying the loan can be a hardship for someone already living in poverty, such as the widows and orphans in the Bible, and can leave them in even greater need than before.

True joy is a gift of the Holy Spirit. It is a feeling that stays with us even if we have problems or troubles. Paul tells us the source of this joy is knowing that we are God's beloved children.

The Pharisees and Sadducees were Jewish religious groups. Pharisees followed the law strictly and did not always love others. The Sadducees thought they were better than others and did not believe in the resurrection.

The word neighbour is related to the word 'nigh' which means 'near.' When Jesus says to love our neighbour, though, he doesn't mean just the people who are close to us—Jesus commands us to love everyone as we love ourselves.

31st Sunday in Ordinary Time

"I am a great King," says the Lord of hosts, "and my name is reverenced among the nations.

"And now, O priests, this command is for you. If you will not listen, if you will not lay it to heart to give glory to my name," says the Lord of hosts, "then I will send the curse on you and I will curse your blessings; indeed I have already cursed them, because you do not lay it to heart.

"You have turned aside from the way; you have caused many to stumble by your instruction; you have corrupted the covenant of Levi," says the Lord of hosts, "and so I make you despised and abased before all the people, inasmuch as you have not kept my ways but have shown partiality in your instruction."

Have we not all one father? Has not one God created us? Why then are we faithless to one another, profaning the covenant of our ancestors?

The word of the Lord. **Thanks be to God.**

Psalm 131

℟. **In you, Lord, I have found my peace.**

O Lord, my heart is not lifted up,
my eyes are not raised too high;
I do not occupy myself with things
too great and too marvellous for me. ℟.

But I have calmed and quieted my soul,
like a weaned child with its mother;
my soul is like the weaned child
that is with me. ℟.

O Israel, hope in the Lord
from this time on and forevermore. ℟.

Brothers and sisters: Though we might have made demands as Apostles of Christ, we were gentle among you, like a nurse tenderly caring for her own children. So deeply do we care for you that we are determined to share with you not only the Gospel of God but also our own selves, because you have become very dear to us. You remember our labour and toil, brothers and sisters; we worked night and day, so that we might not burden any of you while we proclaimed to you the Gospel of God.

We also constantly give thanks to God for this, that when you received the word of God that you heard from us, you accepted it not as a human word but as what it really is, the word of God, which is also at work in you believers.

The word of the Lord. **Thanks be to God.**

Then Jesus said to the crowds and to his disciples, "The scribes and the Pharisees sit in Moses' chair; therefore, do whatever they teach you and follow it; but do not do as they do, for they do not practise what they teach. They tie up heavy burdens, hard to bear, and lay them on the shoulders of others; but they themselves are unwilling to lift a finger to move them. They do all their deeds to be seen by others; for they make their phylacteries broad and their fringes long. They love to have the place of honour at banquets and the best seats in the synagogues, and to be greeted with respect in the marketplaces, and to have people call them rabbi.

"But you are not to be called rabbi, for you have one teacher, and you are all brothers and sisters. And call no one your father on earth, for you have one Father—the one in heaven. Nor are you to be called instructors, for you have one instructor, the Christ. The greatest among you will be your servant. Whoever exalts himself will be humbled, and whoever humbles himself will be exalted."

The Gospel of the Lord. **Praise to you, Lord Jesus Christ.**

The book of the Prophet Malachi tried to awaken hope in the people of Israel at a time when religious practice had deteriorated. It was written 515 years before Christ.

Levi was one of Jacob's twelve sons, and therefore head of one of the twelve tribes of Israel. Levites were of the priestly class and therefore represented the covenant between God and Israel.

When Jesus says that the scribes and Pharisees sit in Moses' chair, he is recognizing that their authority to teach goes back to Moses who received the Ten Commandments from God.

Phylacteries are small boxes worn by Jewish men on the left wrist and on the forehead. The boxes contain biblical texts; they are worn to help the wearer keep God's word always at hand and in mind. Jesus wants us to see that what counts is what is in our heart, and not what we wear on the outside.

32nd Sunday in Ordinary Time

GENINA

Wisdom is radiant and unfading,
and she is easily discerned by those who love her,
and is found by those who seek her.
She hastens to make herself known to those who desire her.
One who rises early to seek her will have no difficulty,
for she will be found sitting at the gate.

To fix one's thought on her is perfect understanding,
and one who is vigilant on her account will soon be free from care,
because she goes about seeking those worthy of her,
and she graciously appears to them in their paths,
and meets them in every thought.

The word of the Lord. **Thanks be to God.**

Psalm 63

R. **My soul thirsts for you, O Lord my God.**

O God, you are my God, I seek you,
my soul thirsts for you;
my flesh faints for you,
as in a dry and weary land where there is no water. R.

So I have looked upon you in the sanctuary,
beholding your power and glory.
Because your steadfast love is better than life,
my lips will praise you. R.

So I will bless you as long as I live;
I will lift up my hands and call on your name.
My soul is satisfied as with a rich feast,
and my mouth praises you with joyful lips. R.

I think of you on my bed,
and meditate on you in the watches of the night;
for you have been my help,
and in the shadow of your wings I sing for joy. R.

A reading from the first Letter of Saint Paul to the Thessalonians (4.13-18)

We do not want you to be uninformed, brothers and sisters, about those who have died, so that you may not grieve as others do who have no hope. For since we believe that Jesus died and rose again, even so, through Jesus, God will bring with him those who have died. For this we declare to you by the word of the Lord, that we who are alive, who are left until the coming of the Lord, will by no means precede those who have died.

For the Lord himself, with a cry of command, with the Archangel's call and with the sound of God's trumpet, will descend from heaven, and the dead in Christ will rise first. Then we who are alive, who are left, will be caught up in the clouds together with them to meet the Lord in the air; and so we will be with the Lord forever. Therefore encourage one another with these words.

The word of the Lord. **Thanks be to God.**

A reading from the holy Gospel according to Matthew (25.1-13)

Jesus spoke this parable to the disciples: "The kingdom of heaven will be like this. Ten bridesmaids took their lamps and went to meet the bridegroom. Five of them were foolish, and five were wise. When the foolish took their lamps, they took no oil with them; but the wise took flasks of oil with their lamps. As the bridegroom was delayed, all of them became drowsy and slept.

"But at midnight there was a shout, 'Look! Here is the bridegroom! Come out to meet him.' Then all those bridesmaids got up and trimmed their lamps. The foolish said to the wise, 'Give us some of your oil, for our lamps are going out.' But the wise replied, 'No! There will not be enough for you and for us; you had better go to the dealers and buy some for yourselves.' And while they went to buy it, the bridegroom came, and those who were ready went with him into the wedding banquet; and the door was shut.

"Later the other bridesmaids came also, saying, 'Lord, lord, open to us.' But he replied, 'Truly I tell you, I do not know you.' Keep awake therefore, for you know neither the day nor the hour."

The Gospel of the Lord. **Praise to you, Lord Jesus Christ.**

The book of Wisdom, in the Bible, was written not long before Jesus was born. It urges us to make good decisions in life. It teaches about justice and fairness.

The sanctuary is the holiest part of the Jewish temple (from the same Latin word for 'holy' that gives us 'saint'). In a church, the sanctuary is the place where the word of God is proclaimed and the eucharist is celebrated.

In the time of Jesus, wedding ceremonies were held at night. Therefore, the bridesmaids needed to have lamps ready to light the way when they went to meet the bridegroom.

The bridesmaids used oil lamps with wicks. The wicks needed to be trimmed properly before lighting so that the lamps would burn brightly, cleanly and not too quickly.

33rd Sunday in Ordinary Time

A capable wife, who can find her?
She is far more precious than jewels.
The heart of her husband trusts in her,
and he will have no lack of gain.
She does him good, and not harm,
all the days of her life.
She seeks wool and flax,
and works with willing hands.

She considers a field and buys it;
with the fruit of her hands she plants a vineyard.
She girds herself with strength,
and makes her arms strong.
She perceives that her merchandise is profitable.
Her lamp does not go out at night.

She opens her hand to the poor,
and reaches out her hands to the needy.
She opens her mouth with wisdom,
and the teaching of kindness is on her tongue.

Her children rise up and call her happy;
her husband too, and he praises her:
"Many women have done excellently,
but you surpass them all."

Charm is deceitful, and beauty is vain,
but a woman who fears the Lord is to be praised.
Give her a share in the fruit of her hands,
and let her works praise her in the city gates.

The word of the Lord. **Thanks be to God.**

R. **Blessed is everyone who fears the Lord.**

Blessed is everyone who fears the Lord,
who walks in his ways.
You shall eat the fruit of the labour of your hands;
you shall be happy, and it shall go well with you. R.

Your wife will be like a fruitful vine
within your house;
your children will be like olive shoots
around your table. R.

Thus shall the man be blessed who fears the Lord.
The Lord bless you from Zion.
May you see the prosperity of Jerusalem
all the days of your life. R.

A reading from the first Letter of Saint Paul to the Thessalonians (5.1-6)

Now concerning the times and the seasons, brothers and sisters, you do not need to have anything written to you. For you yourselves know very well that the day of the Lord will come like a thief in the night. When they say, "There is peace and security," then sudden destruction will come upon them, as labour pains come upon a pregnant woman, and there will be no escape!

But you, beloved, are not in darkness for that day to surprise you like a thief. You are all children of light and children of the day; we are not of the night or of darkness. So then let us not fall asleep as others do, but let us keep awake and be sober.

The word of the Lord. **Thanks be to God.**

For the shorter version, omit the indented parts.

Jesus spoke this parable to his disciples: "For it is as if a man, going on a journey, summoned his slaves and entrusted his property to them; to one he gave five talents, to another two, to another one, to each according to his ability. Then he went away.

> "The one who had received the five talents went off at once and traded with them, and made five more talents. In the same way, the one who had the two talents made two more talents. But the one who had received the one talent went off and dug a hole in the ground and hid his master's money.

"After a long time the master of those slaves came and settled accounts with them. Then the one who had received the five talents came forward, bringing five more talents, saying, 'Master, you handed over to me five talents; see, I have made five more talents.' His master said to him, 'Well done, good and trustworthy slave; you have been trustworthy in a few things, I will put you in charge of many things; enter into the joy of your master.'

> "And the one with the two talents also came forward, saying, 'Master, you handed over to me two talents; see, I have made two more talents. His master said to him, 'Well done, good and trustworthy slave; you have been trustworthy in a few things, I will put you in charge of many things; enter into the joy of your master.'

> "Then the one who had received the one talent also came forward, saying, 'Master, I knew that you were a harsh man, reaping where you did not sow, and gathering where you did not scatter seed; so I was afraid, and I went and hid your talent in the ground. Here you have what is yours.'

281

"But his master replied, 'You wicked and lazy slave! You knew, did you, that I reap where I did not sow, and gather where I did not scatter? Then you ought to have invested my money with the bankers, and on my return I would have received what was my own with interest. So take the talent from him, and give it to the one with the ten talents. For to all those who have, more will be given, and they will have an abundance; but from those who have nothing, even what they have will be taken away. As for this worthless slave, throw him into the outer darkness, where there will be weeping and gnashing of teeth.'"

The Gospel of the Lord. **Praise to you, Lord Jesus Christ.**

KEY WORDS

Proverbs, a book in the Bible, is a collection of popular sayings and parables filled with advice and wisdom.

Wool and flax are two natural materials that are used in making cloth and ropes, both of which were very important in ancient households.

Light is a symbol of everything good and especially of Jesus, who is the light of the world. Darkness represents evil, especially turning away from God.

To live a sober life means to do things in moderation, without excess. If we do not live soberly, then we may be too caught up in our own pleasure and will not pay attention to the needs of others or to the Holy Spirit living within us.

The talents in the parable represent the gifts God has given to each one of us: our intelligence, our memory, our capacity for generosity and kindness. These gifts must be used for the good of all.

To be trustworthy is to be honest and dependable. When someone gives us a task or asks us to keep a secret and we keep our promises, we show that we value that person's friendship.

Christ the King

GENINA

Thus says the Lord God:
"I myself will search for my sheep,
and will seek them out.
As a shepherd seeks out his flock
when he is among his scattered sheep,
so I will seek out my sheep.
I will rescue them from all the places
to which they have been scattered
on a day of clouds and thick darkness.

"I myself will be the shepherd of my sheep,
and I will make them lie down,"
says the Lord God.
"I will seek the lost,
and I will bring back the strayed,
and I will bind up the injured,
and I will strengthen the weak,
but the fat and the strong I will destroy.
I will feed my sheep with justice.

"As for you, my flock," thus says the Lord God:
"I shall judge between one sheep
and another, between rams and goats."

The word of the Lord. **Thanks be to God.**

R. **The Lord is my shepherd; I shall not want.**

The Lord is my shepherd, I shall not want.
He makes me lie down in green pastures;
he leads me beside still waters;
he restores my soul. R.

He leads me in right paths for his name's sake.
Even though I walk through the darkest valley, I fear no evil;
for you are with me;
your rod and your staff—they comfort me. R.

You prepare a table before me
in the presence of my enemies;
you anoint my head with oil;
my cup overflows. R.

Surely goodness and mercy shall follow me
all the days of my life,
and I shall dwell in the house of the Lord
my whole life long. R.

A reading from the first Letter of Saint Paul to the Corinthians (15.20-26, 28)

Brothers and sisters: Christ has been raised from the dead, the first fruits of those who have fallen asleep. For since death came through a man, the resurrection of the dead has also come through a man; for as all die in Adam, so all will be made alive in Christ. But each in his own order: Christ the first fruits, then at his coming those who belong to Christ.

Then comes the end, when he hands over the kingdom to God the Father, after he has destroyed every ruler and every authority and power. For he must reign until he has put all his enemies under his feet. The last enemy to be destroyed is death.

When all things are subjected to him, then the Son himself will also be subjected to the one who put all things in subjection under him, so that God may be all in all.

The word of the Lord. **Thanks be to God.**

Jesus said to his disciples: "When the Son of Man comes in his glory, and all the Angels with him, then he will sit on the throne of his glory. All the nations will be gathered before him, and he will separate people one from another as a shepherd separates the sheep from the goats, and he will put the sheep at his right hand and the goats at the left.

"Then the king will say to those at his right hand, 'Come, you that are blessed by my Father, inherit the kingdom prepared for you from the foundation of the world; for I was hungry and you gave me food, I was thirsty and you gave me something to drink, I was a stranger and you welcomed me, I was naked and you gave me clothing, I was sick and you took care of me, I was in prison and you visited me.'

"Then the righteous will answer him, 'Lord, when was it that we saw you hungry and gave you food, or thirsty and gave you something to drink? And when was it that we saw you a stranger and welcomed you, or naked and gave you clothing? And when was it that we saw you sick or in prison and visited you?' And the king will answer them, 'Truly I tell you, just as you did it to one of the least of these brothers and sisters of mine, you did it to me.'

"Then he will say to those at his left hand, 'You that are accursed, depart from me into the eternal fire prepared for the devil and his angels; for I was hungry and you gave me no food, I was thirsty and you gave me nothing to drink, I was a stranger and you did not welcome me, naked and you did not give me clothing, sick and in prison and you did not visit me.'

"Then they also will answer, 'Lord, when was it that we saw you hungry or thirsty or a stranger or naked or sick or in prison, and did not take care of you?' Then he will answer them, 'Truly I tell you, just as you did not do it to one of the least of these, you did not do it to me.' And these will go away into eternal punishment, but the righteous into eternal life."

The Gospel of the Lord. **Praise to you, Lord Jesus Christ.**

Ezekiel was one of the most important prophets in Israel. He lived during a time when many of the people of Jerusalem were taken prisoner and forced to live in another place, Babylon. The king and Ezekiel were taken away, too. Ezekiel helped the people follow God's ways even though they were far from home.

God calls his people my sheep to show how valuable we are to God. Because they provide wool for clothing as well as meat for food, sheep are very important animals. A community's survival could depend on the safety and health of its sheep.

A shepherd is someone who takes care of a flock of sheep. He would spend days or weeks with his flock, sleeping with them and making sure they were always safe. God loves us with the same constant care.

The Corinthians were a community of Christians who lived in Corinth, a city in Greece. Paul wrote them several letters, two of which are in the Bible.

First fruits were the first crops collected at harvest time. These were offered to God. Paul tells us that Jesus is the first fruits of salvation, the first to die and rise again.

Christ's coming or advent is his return at the end of time. All history is longing for Christ's return, when God's plan of salvation will be complete.

A disciple is a person who follows the teachings of a master and helps to spread these teachings. Jesus was such a master; he had many disciples, including us.

1st Sunday of Advent

You, O Lord, are our father;
"Our Redeemer from of old" is your name.
Why, O Lord, do you make us stray from your ways
and harden our heart, so that we do not fear you?
Turn back for the sake of your servants,
for the sake of the tribes that are your heritage.

O that you would tear open the heavens and come down,
so that the mountains would quake at your presence.
When you did awesome deeds that we did not expect,
you came down, the mountains quaked at your presence.
From ages past no one has heard,
no ear has perceived,
no eye has seen any God besides you,
who works for those who wait for him.

You meet those who gladly do right,
those who remember you in your ways.

But you were angry, and we sinned;
because you hid yourself we transgressed.
We have all become like one who is unclean,
and all our righteous deeds are like a filthy cloth.
We all fade like a leaf,
and our iniquities, like the wind, take us away.
There is no one who calls on your name,
or attempts to take hold of you;
for you have hidden your face from us,
and have delivered us into the hand of our iniquity.

Yet, O Lord, you are our Father;
we are the clay, and you are our potter;
we are all the work of your hand.

The word of the Lord. **Thanks be to God.**

R. **Restore us, O God; let your face shine, that we may be saved.**

Give ear, O Shepherd of Israel,
you who are enthroned upon the cherubim, shine forth.
Stir up your might,
and come to save us. R.

Turn again, O God of hosts;
look down from heaven, and see;
have regard for this vine,
the stock that your right hand has planted. R.

But let your hand be upon the man at your right,
the son of man you have made strong for yourself.
Then we will never turn back from you;
give us life, and we will call on your name. R.

A reading from the first Letter of Saint Paul to the Corinthians (1.3-9)

Brothers and sisters: Grace to you and peace from God our Father and the Lord Jesus Christ.

I give thanks to my God always for you because of the grace of God that has been given you in Christ Jesus, for in every way you have been enriched in him, in speech and knowledge of every kind—just as the testimony of Christ has been strengthened among you—so that you are not lacking in any spiritual gift as you wait for the revealing of our Lord Jesus Christ.

He will also strengthen you to the end, so that you may be blameless on the day of our Lord Jesus Christ. God is faithful; by him you were called into fellowship with his Son, Jesus Christ our Lord.

The word of the Lord. **Thanks be to God.**

Jesus said to his disciples: "Beware, keep alert; for you do not know when the time will come.

"It is like a man going on a journey, when he leaves home and puts his slaves in charge, each with a particular task, and commands the doorkeeper to be on the watch. Therefore, keep awake—for you do not know when the master of the house will come, in the evening, or at midnight, or at cockcrow, or at dawn, or else he may find you asleep when he comes suddenly.

"And what I say to you I say to all: Keep awake."

The Gospel of the Lord. **Praise to you, Lord Jesus Christ.**

With Advent, which means 'coming,' we begin a new liturgical year. The season of Advent lasts four weeks. During this time, the liturgical colour is purple, the colour of waiting, to remind us to prepare our hearts to celebrate the birth of Jesus at Christmas and his return at the end of time.

To redeem is to buy something back or to pay to free someone. God is called Redeemer because God freed Israel from slavery in Egypt. Christ is our Redeemer, for he freed us from the power of death by his resurrection.

When the Bible says that God has hidden his face, it means that sometimes we think God has turned away or is angry. But we know that God is always near and we are the ones who have to turn back to God.

Cherubim (the plural of cherub) are a type of angel. In the Bible they are the ones who watch over the entrance to the Garden of Eden. To show that God is above everything, the psalmist says that God's throne is above the cherubim.

The day of our Lord is the day human history will end and we will see God face to face.

The holy Gospel according to Mark is the earliest and the shortest of the four gospels. It tells the story of some events in Jesus' life to help people know that Jesus is the Son of God.

To beware is to pay attention, to keep watch and to stay awake.

2nd Sunday of Advent

Comfort, O comfort my people,
says your God.
Speak tenderly to Jerusalem,
and cry to her
that she has served her term,
that her penalty is paid,
that she has received from the Lord's hand
double for all her sins.

A voice cries out:
"In the wilderness prepare the way of the Lord,
make straight in the desert a highway for our God.
Every valley shall be lifted up,
and every mountain and hill be made low;
the uneven ground shall become level,
and the rough places a plain.
Then the glory of the Lord shall be revealed,
and all people shall see it together,
for the mouth of the Lord has spoken."

Get you up to a high mountain,
O Zion, herald of good tidings;
lift up your voice with strength,
O Jerusalem, herald of good tidings,
lift it up, do not fear;
say to the cities of Judah,
"Here is your God!"

See, the Lord God comes with might,
and his arm rules for him;
his reward is with him,
and his recompense before him.
He will feed his flock like a shepherd;
he will gather the lambs in his arms,
and carry them in his bosom,
and gently lead the mother sheep.

The word of the Lord. **Thanks be to God.**

R. **Show us your steadfast love, O Lord,**
   and grant us your salvation.

Let me hear what God the Lord will speak,
for he will speak peace to his people.
Surely his salvation is at hand for those who fear him,
that his glory may dwell in our land. R.

Steadfast love and faithfulness will meet;
righteousness and peace will kiss each other.
Faithfulness will spring up from the ground,
and righteousness will look down from the sky. R.

The Lord will give what is good,
and our land will yield its increase.
Righteousness will go before him,
and will make a path for his steps. R.

A reading from the second Letter of Saint Peter (3.8-14)

Do not ignore this one fact, beloved, that with the Lord one day is like a thousand years, and a thousand years are like one day. The Lord is not slow about his promise, as some think of slowness, but is patient with you, not wanting any to perish, but all to come to repentance.

But the day of the Lord will come like a thief, and then the heavens will pass away with a loud noise, and the elements will be dissolved with fire, and the earth and everything that is done on it will be disclosed.

Since all these things are to be dissolved in this way, what sort of persons ought you to be in leading lives of holiness and godliness, waiting for and hastening the coming of the day of God, because of which the heavens will be set ablaze and dissolved, and the elements will melt with fire? But, in accordance with his promise, we wait for new heavens and a new earth, where righteousness is at home.

Therefore, beloved, while you are waiting for these things, strive to be found by him at peace.

The word of the Lord. **Thanks be to God.**

The beginning of the good news of Jesus Christ, the Son of God.

As it is written in the Prophet Isaiah, "See, I am sending my messenger ahead of you, who will prepare your way; the voice of one crying out in the wilderness: 'Prepare the way of the Lord, make his paths straight,'" John the Baptist appeared in the wilderness, proclaiming a baptism of repentance for the forgiveness of sins. And people from the whole Judean countryside and all the people of Jerusalem were going out to him, and were baptized by him in the river Jordan, confessing their sins. Now John was clothed with camel's hair, with a leather belt around his waist, and he ate locusts and wild honey. He proclaimed, "The one who is more powerful than I is coming after me; I am not worthy to stoop down and untie the thong of his sandals. I have baptized you with water; but he will baptize you with the Holy Spirit."

The Gospel of the Lord. **Praise to you, Lord Jesus Christ.**

God does not have a body, but to help us understand God, the Bible uses parts of the human body to describe him: God acts (the Lord's hand), God speaks to us (the mouth of the Lord), God is powerful (his arm rules) and God cares for us (gathers us in his arms).

In the second Letter of Saint Peter, the people are worrying about when Jesus will return. Peter helps them understand that the important thing is to live well and to let God decide when the second coming (or advent) will take place.

Holiness means living near God and letting the Holy Spirit guide us. To be holy is to live in a God-like manner: with love, mercy and compassion.

Prepare the way of the Lord were John the Baptist's words to the people, telling them to change their lives so that they would be ready for the Messiah.

John the Baptist was the son of Zechariah and Elizabeth, a cousin of the Virgin Mary. He told people that Jesus was coming soon. He was called John the Baptist because he baptized many people.

People who are baptized with the Holy Spirit have let God into their lives. The Holy Spirit is alive in them. The apostles received the Holy Spirit on the day of Pentecost. We receive the Holy Spirit in the sacraments of baptism and confirmation.

3rd Sunday of Advent

The spirit of the Lord God is upon me,
because the Lord has anointed me;
he has sent me to bring good news to the oppressed,
to bind up the broken-hearted,
to proclaim liberty to the captives,
and release to the prisoners;
to proclaim the year of the Lord's favour.

I will greatly rejoice in the Lord,
my soul shall exult in my God;
for he has clothed me with the garments of salvation,
he has covered me with the robe of righteousness,
as a bridegroom decks himself with a garland,
and as a bride adorns herself with her jewels.

For as the earth brings forth its shoots,
and as a garden causes what is sown in it to spring up,
so the Lord God will cause righteousness and praise
to spring up before all the nations.

The word of the Lord. **Thanks be to God.**

Luke 1

R. **My soul shall exult in my God.**

My soul magnifies the Lord
and my spirit rejoices in God my Saviour,
for he has looked with favour on the lowliness of his servant.
Surely, from now on all generations will call me blessed. R.

For the Mighty One has done great things for me,
and holy is his name.
His mercy is for those who fear him
from generation to generation. R.

The Lord has filled the hungry with good things
and sent the rich away empty.
He has helped his servant Israel,
in remembrance of his mercy. R.

A reading from the first Letter of Saint Paul to the Thessalonians (5.16-24)

Brothers and sisters, rejoice always, pray without ceasing, give thanks in all circumstances; for this is the will of God in Christ Jesus for you.

Do not quench the Spirit. Do not despise the words of Prophets, but test everything; hold fast to what is good; abstain from every form of evil.

May the God of peace himself sanctify you entirely; and may your spirit and soul and body be kept sound and blameless at the coming of our Lord Jesus Christ. The one who calls you is faithful, and he will do this.

The word of the Lord. **Thanks be to God.**

A reading from the holy Gospel according to John (1.6-8, 19-28)

There was a man sent from God, whose name was John. He came as a witness to testify to the light, so that all might believe through him. He himself was not the light, but he came to testify to the light.

This is the testimony given by John when the Jews sent priests and Levites from Jerusalem to ask him, "Who are you?" He confessed and did not deny it, but confessed, "I am not the Messiah." And they asked him, "What then? Are you Elijah?" He said, "I am not." "Are you the Prophet?" He answered, "No."

Then they said to him, "Who are you? Let us have an answer for those who sent us. What do you say about yourself?" He said, "I am the voice of one crying out in the wilderness, 'Make straight the way of the Lord,'" as the Prophet Isaiah said.

Now they had been sent from the Pharisees. They asked him, "Why then are you baptizing if you are neither the Messiah, nor Elijah, nor the Prophet?" John answered them, "I baptize with water. Among you stands one whom you do not know, the one who is coming after me; I am not worthy to untie the thong of his sandal." This took place in Bethany across the Jordan where John was baptizing.

The Gospel of the Lord. **Praise to you, Lord Jesus Christ.**

To anoint means to 'bless with oil.' In the Bible it can also mean to give someone a mission, an important job. Christians are anointed at baptism and confirmation: our mission is to live as Jesus taught us.

Every 50 years, Israel celebrated a Jubilee Year, a special time when debts were forgiven and wrongs were pardoned. The year of the Lord's favour means that God is offering forgiveness to all those who are sorry for their wrongs and are seeking pardon.

One way to pray is to give thanks to God. We do this, for example, when we say 'grace' before meals—we thank God each day for all the good things God has given us. In many languages, the words for 'grace' and 'thanks' are the same.

In the Gospel according to John, there is another John— John the Baptist, the cousin of Jesus, who preached that everyone had to change their lives and prepare to receive the Messiah.

Jesus and his disciples spoke Aramaic. Messiah is an Aramaic word meaning 'anointed.' The chosen person was anointed or blessed with holy oil and given a special mission. The Greek word for 'anointed' is 'Christ.'

4th Sunday of Advent

Now when David, the king, was settled in his house, and the Lord had given him rest from all his enemies around him, the king said to the Prophet Nathan, "See now, I am living in a house of cedar, but the ark of God stays in a tent." Nathan said to the king, "Go, do all that you have in mind, for the Lord is with you."

But that same night the word of the Lord came to Nathan: "Go and tell my servant David: 'Thus says the Lord: Are you the one to build me a house to live in? I took you from the pasture, from following the sheep to be prince over my people Israel: and I have been with you wherever you went, and have cut off all your enemies from before you; and I will make for you a great name, like the name of the great ones of the earth.

"And I will appoint a place for my people Israel and will plant them, so that they may live in their own place, and be disturbed no more; and evildoers shall afflict them no more, as formerly, from the time that I appointed judges over my people Israel; and I will give you rest from all your enemies.

"Moreover the Lord declares to you, David, that the Lord will make you a house. When your days are fulfilled and you lie down with your ancestors, I will raise up your offspring after you, who shall come forth from your body, and I will establish his kingdom.

"I will be a father to him, and he shall be a son to me. Your house and your kingdom shall be made sure forever before me; your throne, David, shall be established forever.'"

The word of the Lord. **Thanks be to God.**

R̰ **Forever I will sing of your steadfast love, O Lord.**

I will sing of your steadfast love, O Lord, forever;
with my mouth I will proclaim your faithfulness
    to all generations.
I declare that your steadfast love is established forever;
your faithfulness is as firm as the heavens. R̰

You said, "I have made a covenant with my chosen one,
I have sworn to my servant David:
I will establish your descendants forever,
and build your throne for all generations." R̰

He shall cry to me, "You are my Father,
my God, and the Rock of my salvation!"
Forever I will keep my steadfast love for him,
and my covenant with him will stand firm. R̰

A reading from the Letter of Saint Paul to the Romans (16.25-27)

Brothers and sisters: To the One who is able to strengthen you according to my Gospel and the proclamation of Jesus Christ, according to the revelation of the mystery that was kept secret for long ages but is now disclosed, and through the prophetic writings is made known to all the Gentiles, according to the command of the eternal God, to bring about the obedience of faith—to the only wise God, through Jesus Christ, to whom be the glory forever! Amen.

The word of the Lord. **Thanks be to God.**

The Angel Gabriel was sent by God to a town in Galilee called Nazareth, to a virgin engaged to a man whose name was Joseph, of the house of David. The virgin's name was Mary.

And he came to her and said, "Hail, full of grace! The Lord is with you." But she was much perplexed by his words and pondered what sort of greeting this might be.

The Angel said to her, "Do not be afraid, Mary, for you have found favour with God. And now, you will conceive in your womb and bear a son, and you will name him Jesus.

"He will be great, and will be called the Son of the Most High, and the Lord God will give to him the throne of his father David. He will reign over the house of Jacob forever, and of his kingdom there will be no end."

Mary said to the Angel, "How can this be, since I am a virgin?" The Angel said to her, "The Holy Spirit will come upon you, and the power of the Most High will overshadow you; therefore the child to be born will be holy; he will be called Son of God.

"And now, your relative Elizabeth in her old age has also conceived a son; and this is the sixth month for her who was said to be barren. For nothing will be impossible with God." Then Mary said, "Here am I, the servant of the Lord; let it be done to me according to your word." Then the Angel departed from her.

The Gospel of the Lord.
Praise to you, Lord Jesus Christ.

Samuel, a prophet and judge in Israel, was born over 1,000 years before Jesus. The Lord chose Samuel to anoint the first king of Israel, Saul. He also anointed David, who was king after Saul. The Bible contains two books in his name: 1 Samuel and 2 Samuel.

The ark of God, also called the ark of the covenant, was a wooden box in which the Israelites stored important objects that reminded them that God was their saviour. It was built to contain the two stone tablets on which the Ten Commandments were written, a golden urn of manna (the miraculous bread that fell from heaven when the Israelites were living in the desert) and Aaron's staff.

Before he was anointed king of Israel, David was a lowly shepherd. It was by God's grace that David was chosen and not because of anything special David had done to earn the title. When God tells David that "I took you from the pasture," God is reminding him that it is God who chooses, not David.

A mystery is something that is very hard to understand. In Paul's Letter to the Romans, mystery refers to God's plan to create a human community in Christ.

The holy Gospel according to Luke was written for people who, like Luke, weren't Jewish before becoming Christian. This gospel tells the most about Mary, the mother of Jesus.

When the gospel says that Mary and Joseph were engaged, it means that they had promised to marry each other.

The gospel assures us that Joseph was descended from the house of David. This fulfills the promise made by the prophets that the Messiah would be born from among David's descendants.

Christmas
The Nativity of the Lord

GENINA

The people who walked in darkness have seen a great light;
those who lived in a land of deep darkness—
on them light has shone.
You have multiplied the nation,
you have increased its joy;
they rejoice before you
as with joy at the harvest,
as people exult when dividing plunder.

For the yoke of their burden,
and the bar across their shoulders,
the rod of their oppressor,
you have broken as on the day of Midian.

For a child has been born for us,
a son given to us;
authority rests upon his shoulders;
and he is named
Wonderful Counsellor, Mighty God,
Everlasting Father, Prince of Peace.

His authority shall grow continually,
and there shall be endless peace
for the throne of David and his kingdom.
He will establish and uphold it
with justice and with righteousness
from this time onward and forevermore.
The zeal of the Lord of hosts will do this.

The word of the Lord. **Thanks be to God.**

GENINA

R. **Today is born our Saviour, Christ the Lord.**

O sing to the Lord a new song;
sing to the Lord, all the earth.
Sing to the Lord, bless his name;
tell of his salvation from day to day. R.

Declare his glory among the nations,
his marvellous works among all the peoples.
For great is the Lord, and greatly to be praised;
he is to be revered above all gods. R.

Let the heavens be glad, and let the earth rejoice;
let the sea roar, and all that fills it;
let the field exult, and everything in it.
Then shall all the trees of the forest sing for joy. R.

Rejoice before the Lord; for he is coming,
for he is coming to judge the earth.
He will judge the world with righteousness,
and the peoples with his truth. R.

A reading from the Letter of Saint Paul to Titus
(2.11-14)

Beloved: The grace of God has appeared, bringing salvation to all, training us to renounce impiety and worldly passions, and in the present age to live lives that are self-controlled, upright, and godly, while we wait for the blessed hope and the manifestation of the glory of our great God and Saviour, Jesus Christ.

He it is who gave himself for us that he might redeem us from all iniquity and purify for himself a people of his own who are zealous for good deeds.

The word of the Lord. **Thanks be to God.**

In those days a decree went out from Caesar Augustus that all the world should be registered. This was the first registration and was taken while Quirinius was governor of Syria. All went to their own towns to be registered. Joseph also went from the town of Nazareth in Galilee to Judea, to the city of David called Bethlehem, because he was descended from the house and family of David. He went to be registered with Mary, to whom he was engaged and who was expecting a child.

While they were there, the time came for her to deliver her child. And she gave birth to her firstborn son and wrapped him in swaddling clothes, and laid him in a manger, because there was no place for them in the inn.

In that region there were shepherds living in the fields, keeping watch over their flock by night. Then an Angel of the Lord stood before them, and the glory of the Lord shone around them, and they were terrified. But the Angel said to them, "Do not be afraid; for see—I am bringing you good news of great joy for all the people: to you is born this day in the city of David a Saviour, who is the Christ, the Lord. This will be a sign for you: you will find a child wrapped in swaddling clothes and lying in a manger."

And suddenly there was with the Angel a multitude of the heavenly host, praising God and saying, "Glory to God in the highest heaven, and on earth peace among those whom he favours!"

When the Angels had left them and gone into heaven, the shepherds said to one another, "Let us go now to Bethlehem and see this thing that has taken place, which the Lord has made known to us." So they went with haste and found Mary and Joseph, and the child lying in the manger.

The Gospel of the Lord. **Praise to you, Lord Jesus Christ.**

To exult is to be extremely happy.

A yoke is a heavy harness, usually made of wood, which ties oxen to a plough. Wearing such a thing would be awkward and uncomfortable. The coming of Jesus is thus compared to the lifting of a great burden from a suffering humanity.

To be revered is to be held in the highest esteem. We revere God because he loves us and does mighty things for us.

Grace is the action of the Spirit in the lives of people and in God's creation. By the gift of grace we become better followers of Jesus.

A decree was an order from the Roman ruler of that time. It had to be obeyed.

Syria is a country in the Middle East, which borders Israel and Lebanon. In the time of Jesus, the ruler of Syria was responsible for this entire region.

A manger is a wooden crate where hay is placed to feed the animals in a stable. The baby Jesus was placed in a manger soon after he was born. This was an amazing thing: that God would choose to be born in such a stark and humble manner.

Glory to God in the highest and on earth peace to all people!

Merry Christmas!

Morning Prayers

A Child's Prayer for Morning

Now, before I run to play,
let me not forget to pray
to God who kept me through the night
and waked me with the morning light.
Help me, Lord, to love you more
than I have ever loved before.
In my work and in my play
please be with me through the day.
Amen.

Morning Prayer

Dear God, we thank you for this day.
We thank you for our families and friends.
We thank you for our classmates.
Be with us as we work and play today.
Help us always to be kind to each other.
We pray in the name of the Father,
and of the Son and of the Holy Spirit. Amen.

(Heather Reid, *Let's Pray! Prayers for the Elementary Classroom*. Ottawa; Novalis: 2006)

Angel of God

Angel of God, my guardian dear,
to whom God's love entrusts me here,
ever this day be at my side,
to light and guard, to rule and guide. Amen.

Evening Prayers

Children's Bedtime Prayer

Now I lay me down to sleep,
I pray you, Lord, your child to keep.
Your love will guard me through the night
and wake me with the morning light. Amen.

Child's Evening Prayer

I hear no voice, I feel no touch,
I see no glory bright;
but yet I know that God is near,
in darkness as in light.
He watches ever by my side,
and hears my whispered prayer:
the Father for his little child
both night and day does care.

God Hear My Prayer

God in heaven hear my prayer,
keep me in your loving care.
Be my guide in all I do,
bless all those who love me too. Amen.

Mealtime Prayers

Grace before Meals

Bless us, O Lord,
and these your gifts
which we are about to receive
from your bounty.
Through Christ our Lord. Amen.

* * *

For food in a world where many walk in hunger,
for friends in a world where many walk alone,
for faith in a world where many walk in fear,
we give you thanks, O God. Amen.

* * *

God is great, God is good!
Let us thank God for our food. Amen.

* * *

Be present at our table, Lord.
Be here and everywhere adored.
Your creatures bless
and grant that we may feast
in paradise with you. Amen.

Grace after Meals

We give you thanks, Almighty God,
for these and all the benefits
we receive from your bounty.
Through Christ our Lord. Amen.

* * *

Blessed be the name of the Lord.
Now and forever. Amen.

Traditional Prayers

Lord's Prayer

Our Father, who art in heaven,
hallowed be thy name;
thy kingdom come;
thy will be done on earth as it is in heaven.
Give us this day our daily bread;
and forgive us our trespasses
as we forgive those who trespass against us;
and lead us not into temptation,
but deliver us from evil. Amen.

Hail Mary

Hail Mary, full of grace,
the Lord is with you.
Blessed art you among women and
blessed is the fruit of your womb, Jesus.
Holy Mary, Mother of God,
pray for us sinners,
now and the hour of our death. Amen.

Glory Be to the Father

Glory be to the Father,
and to the Son,
and to the Holy Spirit.
As it was in the beginning,
is now, and ever shall be,
world without end. Amen.

More Prayers

Prayer for Friends

Loving God, you are the best friend we can have.

We ask today that you help us to be good friends
    to each other.

Help us to be fair, kind and unselfish.

Keep our friends safe and happy.

Bless us and bless all friends in this community.

We pray in the name of Jesus,

who was always the friend of children. Amen.

(Heather Reid, *Let's Pray! Prayers for the Elementary Classroom.*
Ottawa; Novalis: 2006)

In the Silence

If we really want to pray,
we must first learn to listen,
for in the silence of the heart,
God speaks.
(Blessed Teresa of Calcutta, 1910-1997)

Family Prayer

Father, what love you have given us.
May we love as you would have us love.
Teach us to be kind to each other,
patient and gentle with one another.
Help us to bear all things together,
to see in our love, your love,
through Christ our Lord. Amen.

Prayer for the Birthday Child

May God bless you with every good gift
and surround you with love and happiness.
May Jesus be your friend and guide
all the days of your life.
May the Spirit of God guide your footsteps
in the path of truth. Amen.

Prayer for Pets

Dear Father, hear and bless
your beasts and singing birds,
and guard with care and tenderness
small things that have no words. Amen.

When Someone Has Died

Lord God, hear our cries.
Grant us comfort in our sadness,
gently wipe away our tears,
and give us courage in the days ahead.
We ask this through Christ our Lord. Amen.

Palestine 2,000 years ago

When Jesus lived here…

- Palestine was a small country, occupied by soldiers of the Roman Empire. Jerusalem was the capital city.
- The country already had a very long history. It was in a part of the world we call the "cradle of civilization."
- Travellers from all around the Mediterranean Sea and the Far East passed through Palestine. Neighbours and visitors included Egyptians, Phoenicians, Syrians, Parthians, Nabateans, Greeks and many others.
- Many citizens understood several languages, including Aramaic, Hebrew, Greek and Latin.

Three horizontal divisions:

- North: Galilee (area #2 on the map) is an area of pleasant weather. Jesus spent most of his life here.
- Central: Samaria (area #3) reaches from the sea coast to the mountain range.
- South: Judea (area #1) is a mountainous region with harsh, dry weather.

Four geographic regions (vertical strips):

- The coastal plain: a broad, flat section along the coast, wide in the south and narrower in the north. Summers here are hot and humid.
- The mountain chain: dry and desert in the south; more fertile valleys in the north.
- The deep ravine: the Jordan Rift Valley splits the mountain range in two, with the Sea of Galilee at one end of the rift and the Jordan River flowing south to the Dead Sea at the other end.
- The plateau: a high, flat area beyond the mountains on the east side of the Jordan River.

Palestine today:

Most of the country where Jesus lived is now called 'Israel.' It is bordered by Lebanon to the north, Syria and Jordan to the east, and Egypt to the south.

1. Judea	5. Perea
2. Galilee	6. Decapolis
3. Samaria	7. Syria and Tetrarchy of Philip
4. Phoenicia	8. Idumea

EGYPT